BEGINNERS QUICK START INTO THE SPORT WITH EASE

The SIMPLE HUNTING *Guide*

TRACKING, SCOUTING, AND SURVIVAL SKILLS

PAT GATZ

© Copyright 2021 - All rights reserved.

The content contained within this book may not be reproduced, duplicated or transmitted without direct written permission from the author or the publisher.

Under no circumstances will any blame or legal responsibility be held against the publisher, or author, for any damages, reparation, or monetary loss due to the information contained within this book, either directly or indirectly.

Legal Notice:
This book is copyright protected. It is only for personal use. You cannot amend, distribute, sell, use, quote or paraphrase any part, or the content within this book, without the consent of the author or publisher.

Disclaimer Notice:
Please note the information contained within this document is for educational and entertainment purposes only. All effort has been executed to present accurate, up to date, reliable, complete information. No warranties of any kind are declared or implied. Readers acknowledge that the author is not engaged in the rendering of legal, financial, medical or professional advice. The content within this book has been derived from various sources. Please consult a licensed professional before attempting any techniques outlined in this book.

By reading this document, the reader agrees that under no circumstances is the author responsible for any losses, direct or indirect, that are incurred as a result of the use of the information contained within this document, including, but not limited to, errors, omissions, or inaccuracies.

Interior Design by FomattedBooks

CONTENTS

Introduction ix

CHAPTER 1: BASIC HUNTER EDUCATION 1
    Hunter's Education 2
    Weapon Licenses and Courses 4
        General Firearm Safety Tips 5
    License to Hunt 6
    Other Permits 8
    What Can You Do Once You Have a License? 9
    Where May I Hunt? 10

CHAPTER 2: PRACTICAL SURVIVAL EQUIPMENT AND GEAR 14
    Hunting Gear 15
    Hunting Attire 18
    Vital Extras 20
    Possible Hunting Weapons 23
        Snares and Traps 24
        Slingshots 26
            Making a Slingshot 27
        Pellet Guns 29
        .410 Bore 30
        .22 Long Rifle (.22 LR) 31

CHAPTER 3: HOW TO SURVIVE—WHAT EVERY HUNTER MUST KNOW 33
- Getting Lost 34
- Now What? 35
  - Shelter 35
  - Water 39
  - Fire 41
  - Food 48

CHAPTER 4: SMALL GAME FOR STARTERS 52
- Squirrel 53
- Rabbit 55
- Grouse 57
- Partridge 58
- Quail 60
- Ducks 61
- Turkey 62
- Bullfrog 64
- Snapping Turtle 66
- Larger Prey 67
  - Deer 67
  - Moose 67
  - Bear 68
  - Wolf 68

CHAPTER 5: IDENTIFYING SIGNS AND TRACKS 69
- Age of Tracks 70
- When to Track 70
- Squirrel 71
- Rabbit 72
- Upland Birds 73
- Ducks 74

Turkey 75
Bullfrog 77
Snapping Turtle 78
Other Possible Signs... 79

CHAPTER 6: BETTER SCOUT MORE THAN YOU HUNT 81
Scouting From a Distance 82
Scouting off-Season 83
Scouting While Hunting 84
Squirrels 86
Rabbits 87
Upland Birds 89
    Grouse 89
    Partridge 90
    Quail 91
Ducks 91
Turkey 93
Bullfrog 95
Snapping Turtle 96

CHAPTER 7: PRACTICE MAKES A MASTER 98
How to Be a Better Hunter 98
Sharpening Specific Skills 102
    Bird Calls 102
    Making Snares 103
    Setting Snares 105
    Making and Setting a Deadfall Trap 108
    Shooting Practice 110

CHAPTER 8: DOMINATE YOUR FIRST HUNT **112**
    Preparing Before the Hunt 112
    Preparing Yourself for a Hunt 115
    Preparing the Hunt 116
    Going Bigger 118

Conclusion 121
References 125
    Image References 136

A SPECIAL GIFT TO OUR READERS!

Included with your purchase of this book is our Field Dressing Starters Guide. This guide will prepare you with some essential critical tips not to forget when you start field dressing small game. It has a secret golden nugget at the end, too!

Click the link below and let us know which email address to deliver it to.

www.patgatz.com

INTRODUCTION

No matter where we are in the world, we generally know where our food comes from. Fruits, vegetables, and meat (in all its varieties) come from farms before it arrives in the shops and lastly upon our plates. We are not truly in control of where our food comes from. Or are we? Some people go away for a few days a year and return with their freezers bursting with fresh meat. However, this meat wasn't simply picked up at a bulk sale. No, this meat was earned through dedication, hard work, and the ability to be patient. These people spend weeks gathering the necessary information, licenses, and equipment before traveling to get this meat. They earn it through hunting.

Why try hunting if your food can be bought at any corner store? It is simple. It isn't just about food. Yes, hunting is a way to replenish your meat stocks before winter, as well as a way for you to control where your food comes from, but it is so much more than just that. It's about getting out into nature and seeing what there is to see. It's a way to experience animals in their natural habitat and a way to protect them through conservation. A hunter doesn't go into the forest to kill. They go to harvest and make use of the animal they are looking for. A true hunter never wastes any animal, be it a squirrel, a fish, a rabbit, or even a moose. Hunting for the pot allows you to have a varied diet beyond what is simply available to you in a grocery store.

When you look at a hunter, you may expect to see a rugged, hardy person (with an excessive number of guns and knives) who is willing to do whatever they must to get their quarry. This leaves many people considering hunting, feeling that they can never live up to that standard that they believe a hunter should be. Yet, it is essential to note that no one is a *standard* hunter, and anyone can hunt. Yes, anyone can hunt. Whether you are an I.T. expert, a stay-at-home parent, or a CEO of a major company, you can hunt. Anyone can hunt. Even children who can pick up a slingshot can hunt small game. It is a simple practice but comes with great responsibility.

So, if you have found yourself sitting at your desk or home and aimlessly staring out into the distance wondering if you, yes you, can try your hand at hunting, know this: Yes, you can! With *The Simple Hunting Guide: Beginners Quick Start Into The Sport With Ease - Tracking, Scouting, And Survival Skills*, getting into hunting has never been simpler. This book aims to get you to start your first hunt with all the necessary information that you will ever need.

This essential hunter's guide contains everything from teaching you about the basics of hunter's education, firearm safety (if you will be using this kind of hunting tool), what kinds of prey are available to you, and the method. That means how you will harvest the animal, be it a bow, pellet gun, rifle, or even slingshot. See? You are already learning.

A hunter should always be prepared. You cannot just picture the result of your hunt because that is only the final step. You need to take several steps before setting foot into the location you will be hunting in. You will learn which tools are best suited for your particular hunt and what is needed to get the best from your outing.

However, what happens if something terrible happens? Prepare for the worst, and you will never be caught off guard. Learn about not only the animals you seek to harvest but also their predators. Start by practicing your skills on the smaller game before moving onto the larger animals. This will help you build confidence and sharpen your skills as you set your target on larger game. Each animal is different, and tracking them through their behavior and tracks is a vital skill to have, which this book offers.

By being fully prepared to enter the unknown, you will be able to tackle even the stickiest of situations where you may be forced to survive a few days out in the wilderness. I did say it's possible to become a hunter, not that it will be an easy feat. Hunting isn't just about loading a weapon and shooting the first animal you see. There is a lot to learn before you should even consider starting a hunt. Luckily, you have picked up the right book to help you through your beginner phase and become a veteran hunter.

Hunting is in everyone's blood, as this is how our ancestors lived before they settled and started to farm. We should all be able to return to the hunter-gatherer way if we are so inclined to. My name is Pat Gatz, and I am a native of Northern Ontario. This area is known for its dense forests and thick marshes for as far as the eye can see and even beyond that. This was where my wolf pack of siblings and I learned about respecting and gathering what we could from nature. As soon as I was old enough to hold a slingshot, I was hunting partridge, snakes, and any other animal that crossed my path. I was only three years old. There was no book out there to help me understand hunting and a collection of people who handed down their knowledge to make the best of my developing hunting skills.

I have been hunting for over 20 years. I have come to treat this activity not only as a sport but as a way for one to connect with nature, find inner peace, and find happiness while respecting the life around me. With so many years of hunting, I have found that it is time to hand down the knowledge presented to me as a youngster to the newer generation (new to hunting and not an age-related issue). My goal is to make sure that your very first hunt and sequential hunts after that go flawlessly, and you succeed in bagging your quarry time and time again.

Hunting is truly a primal skill that everyone will have a calling to at some point in their lives, and with this book at your side, you will be able to follow through with that call. Whether you hunt for the pot or trophies, may this book guide you with the knowledge that has taken me years to gather. Once you have completed this book, you will have an appreciation for hunting as a sport—one that is easy to get into once you are fully prepared. Dive into this hunting grail, a complete beginner's hunting know-how manual, to discover the joy of being out in the wilderness, stalking your prey while respecting it at the same time. There is simply no time like the present to pick up a new sport that will allow you the freedom that so many people long for; it will amass you fresh meat that will make your family and friends jealous at all the cookouts. Hunting is in your blood, so open this book and start your training to sharpen those dormant skills. Hunt to live, live to hunt!

CHAPTER 1

BASIC HUNTER EDUCATION

To improve at anything in life, you need to have a basic understanding and further education in that specific area. This holds very true to hunting. Before one can get a weapon to use in harvesting animals, you will need to understand what goes into hunting and how you can remain within the laws of your respective state/province. In the provinces of Canada and the states of America, there are vastly different laws involved in hunting and owning any kind of firearm. It is your responsibility to ensure that you know the laws of your respective area and where you will be hunting to ensure what documentation you may need to complete hunts in those areas. Since these areas are so vastly different, an overview of what to do and ask for will be presented in this chapter. When in doubt, it is a good idea to contact your state or province's specific—or the state/province you will be hunting in—Fish and Wildlife Service Department to get the answers to any of your questions.

HUNTER'S EDUCATION

Many places in America and Canada require that a person undergo an education course, known as Hunter Ed, before allowing them to get a license for hunting. This is an essential course for all those starting as the basics of hunting, gun safety, and various other aspects are covered to ensure that responsible hunters are going out into the world. Upon completing this kind of course, you will be presented with a National Hunter Education certificate and a Hunter Safety card that states that you have completed the course. This certificate should be accepted in any jurisdiction as long as the International Hunter Education Association—USA (IHEA-USA) requirements are met. This is called reciprocity and can also hold for various gun permits that may be needed. Before signing up and completing any Hunter Ed course, make sure that the IHEA-USA endorses them.

Hunter Ed is important in teaching you about gun safety and other safety tips to keep you safe when hunting in the wilderness. Other aspects of the course will include how to behave responsibly in nature. You are there to hunt, not poach. Know the hunting laws and the state/province laws to ensure that you conserve the natural environment, respect other hunters and the wildlife, and always make a clean kill. The course will also provide you with copious amounts of knowledge of applying yourself during a hunt and pointing out acceptable behavior while on a hunt. Lastly, the course also encourages that the new hunter becomes involved in hunting groups and conservation organizations. This means that you learn to work together with wardens and private landowners to preserve habitats and wildlife. Being a hunter isn't just about harvesting animals. It is also about managing wildlife and respecting the nature that you find yourself in.

The goal of Hunter Ed is to train safety-conscious, responsible, and law-abiding hunters. These courses are generally aimed at those new to hunting but make great refresher courses for those considered veteran hunters. By completing this course, you will promote responsible hunting behavior, become aware and abide by the different hunting laws and regulations, and lower the risk of hunting accidents while increasing your safety while you hunt.

If you find yourself wanting to hunt in a state/province that doesn't require a Hunter Ed certificate because of age or other factors, go ahead and complete it anyway. There is no downside to completing the course and so many benefits to having it, especially if you plan to use a firearm in your hunting. Hunter Ed can be completed online, in room, and field tested, so see for yourself which method you prefer and apply today! A Hunter Ed course can vary from free to upward of $30, so shop around for the course that best suits you, but ensure that it is compliant with all the regulations of the IHEA-USA (Krebs, 2020). Once you are certified, you never have to go through this course again unless you want to attend a refresher course. Remember to make copies of your card and certificate, and keep them in a safe place. It is also a good idea to keep your Hunter Ed number on your phone for safekeeping.

WEAPON LICENSES AND COURSES

Suppose you are planning to use firearms in your hunting travels. It is an excellent idea to make sure of the respective gun laws between the different states/provinces. What holds in one state/province may not be true in another, and you do not want to end up in hot water because of it. Although some states/provinces share reciprocity in terms of gun permits, this may not be true for others. Due to this, when you are traveling for hunting to a different state/province, you will need to ensure that you have the correct permits for your weapons or you may stand a chance of having them confiscated and being arrested!

It is strongly suggested that you take the time to become acquainted with the weapon you will be using to harvest on a hunt. There are many gun safety courses you can take to become certified in using a gun. (Tip: This is not always a requirement for getting your hunting license but a general safety suggestion.) Understanding and respecting a weapon makes it a valuable tool in the hands of the one handling it instead of a deadly implement that can have dire consequences when mishandled.

Although many states/provinces do not require you to have completed a bowhunter course, if you have completed Hunter Ed course, states like New York and Montana do. Due to this, always check before going on a hunt to avoid unnecessary fines.

General Firearm Safety Tips

Firearms are dangerous. They can and will kill, both intentionally and unintentionally. Understanding the safety involved with these hunting tools is what makes you not only an excellent hunter but one that will avoid harming themselves or others unintentionally. Here are some general tips that will help you with handling your hunting tool responsibly:

- Before making use of the weapon, ensure that the barrel is clean and clear of all obstructions.
- Use the correct ammunition with the weapon.
- Do not store the ammunition with the weapon.
- When the weapon is not in use, clear it of all ammunition.
- No running, climbing, or jumping with a loaded gun. There could be a misfire.
- No drinking of alcohol before or during a hunt.
- Only point the muzzle of a gun at its intended animal quarry and nothing else. Not even as a joke.
- Treat all guns as if they are loaded, period.
- Keep the safety on until you are ready to take a shot.
- Before firing at your target, be sure to know what is in front of it as well as behind it. Bullets can travel farther than most people think.
- Never rest your finger on the trigger. Keep it on the trigger guard until you are ready to take the shot.

Although many of these tips seem obvious for hunting when one is overconfident, you tend to forget the rules and make mistakes. If you are lucky, this kind of mistake will only cost you your quarry. If you are not, this will spell the end of your hunting adventure, one way or another.

LICENSE TO HUNT

You are now almost ready to get a license to hunt. Before you can get your license, you need to ask yourself what, when, where, and how. What are you going to hunt? Are you considering going after big game, predators, or small game? When will you go hunting? Some animals can only hunt at certain times of the year to avoid overhunting or possible pregnancies. You will need a general hunting license if you want to hunt these animals while in season. If for some reason you cannot hunt these animals within their hunting season, you will need to apply to get a special permit to hunt them outside of the allotted season. Where will you go hunting? Where you are from may not have the animal you wish to hunt. Research where this animal could be found and then get the necessary documentation ready to hunt that animal in its respective state/province. Keep in mind that some states like Colorado and California have a lottery system that awards hunting permits for certain large game, and there is no guarantee they will pick you. Some states and provinces will also be divided into different sections. You need to be sure that you are hunting in the correct area or fines may be possible.

How will you hunt? This is a crucial question you need to ask yourself. If you are not comfortable with firearms, there is no need to make use of them. There are several animals you can hunt with a bow during bow season. These include black bears, mule deer, and even elk. Keep in mind that rules determine what kind of bow or crossbow you are allowed to use during the different hunting seasons. If you prefer the smaller game, you can use snares, slingshots, or even pellet guns, as long as you are in season to do so and legal in the state or province. It is essential to look at what animal you will be hunting and the terrain you have access to. This will also help you determine which method of taking is best.

Now that you have answered all the questions, you can move along to getting your hunting license for the state/province you wish to hunt in. If you will be hunting with children or are not quite an adult yet, be aware of the age restrictions in the various states and provinces. If you are old enough to hunt, ensure that a parent gives consent to you doing so, as some states/provinces will not allow a minor to hunt without this. You will also need a valid form of identification to prove who you are. Be sure to have nothing against your name, such as outstanding fines or taxes, as this can prevent you from getting a license until it's paid in full. You may be asked to present your Hunter's Safety card as proof that you have completed Hunter Ed. Lastly, you will need to cover the costs associated with the license you wish to purchase. Each state/province will have its costs as well as different kinds of licenses that will be available. Some licenses only last for the hunting season, a year, or could be for a lifetime. Some licenses can even be extended or have days changed if you cannot make it for whatever reason. Contact the respective Fish and Game Department for that state/province to find out more about their various rules and regulations.

A website like <u>Reserve America</u> can help you get everything ready for the various hunting licenses you may need for the state or province you want to hunt, trap, or fish in. Once you have your license, you will be able to hunt most small game. However, suppose you are interested in a specific animal. In that case, you may need to purchase special tags or permits to go along with your hunting license. You can buy over-the-counter tags—which will allow you to hunt specific animals like deer or turkeys—or you can purchase draw tags. Draw tags are for high-demand animals but may not have the numbers to support the demand. There is a limited number of these tags, so it comes down to first come, first served, or a lottery system to see who is awarded these tags. If you prefer hunting migratory birds, you will have to purchase a yearly duck stamp that will allow you to do so.

OTHER PERMITS

If you want to hunt on public land, you will need to have a pass to access those lands. The most accessible pass covering most public areas where you may want to hunt is "America the Beautiful—The National Parks and Federal Recreational Lands Pass Series. Except for about 30 refuges with extra costs—such as entrance fees or parking fees—this pass allows a car of four individuals over the age of 16 entrance into most national parks. These passes help with the park's upkeep, covers your entrance fee, and allows for amenities to be maintained. Not all parks allow hunting, so make sure before you plan a hunt in your favorite hiking area!

This pass is renewable every year for about $80 for most people, while those in the military can pick it up for free. Seniors can get a lifetime pass for $80 or pay a yearly fee of $20. Those with a permanent disability—though this person doesn't have to be 100% disabled—can get the pass for free. Keep in mind that there may be extra costs involved in processing the ordering of this pass online. Still, it is worth having in the long run, especially if you are scoping the area for a possible hunt later in the season.

WHAT CAN YOU DO ONCE YOU HAVE A LICENSE?

Once you have your license, this doesn't mean that there aren't rules that you need to follow. Each state/province has its regulations and guidelines that you will need to follow or face various penalties. When hunting, only do so within the scope of the license you purchased. Don't hunt deer when you are not carrying a license to do so. Only hunt the approved animals at the correct place and time of the year. Follow the state/province requirements for the number of animals that can be harvested, as there are usually limits. If you are hunting big game, remember to tag your kills before dressing them for travel.

Failure to uphold these regulations could result in revoking your license for a limited period or permanently, fines, or even jail time. Follow what you were taught in Hunter Ed and be a conscientious hunter. Make sure that you stay up to date with all possible regulations every year.

If you find that you are not ready to fire a weapon, then consider going along on some hunts where you can learn from a mentor. It is from these people that you can pick up the tricks of the trade. They already know the animal's movements, what to look for when hunting certain animals, and how to avoid being spotted. You need to build up experience that doesn't always come from hunting yourself, so don't be afraid to look for a mentor to help you. Ensure that you have all the right equipment and be well versed in using all of it. If you haven't practiced using a gun, then you shouldn't be using it. Know what kind of clothing you should be wearing and if you need to be visible to other possible hunters.

WHERE MAY I HUNT?

Once you are fully licensed and have all other necessary documents ready, then the next thing you need to decide is what kind of land you will hunt on. There are only two possibilities: public or private. Regardless of which you hunt on, you will need to check the state or province's regulations to see if anything may be required on your part to hunt on these two lands.

If you aim to hunt on public land, you can do so as the state/province regulates hunting. There will be clear areas marked out for where you may and may not hunt, since everyone shares this land. This includes people who are hiking, camping, and bird watching. You will need to make sure that you get to know the land and come prepared with any equipment you may need on your hunts.

Public lands that are huntable include national wildlife refuges, Bureau of Land Management (BLM) managed public lands, as well as national preserves (U.S. Department of the Interior, 2017). As long as these are huntable lands and you have permission to be there, you may hunt for what your license allows you to.

Hunting on private land can become a little tricky as there are ever-changing laws—depending on which state or province you are in—surrounding this type of hunting. If a friend invites you to hunt on his property, you may not necessarily need a license. Still, a license is required if the property belongs to someone else. Not all states/provinces have public areas to hunt on, but there is an abundance of privately owned land that contains all manners of animals that may be hunted if the landowner allows it. This is where the rights of two specific types of people—landowners and hunters—have come under fire in recent years.

If a hunter stumbles onto land that has no post that states either "No Trespassing" or "No Entry," the consensus is that the property allows entrance for hunters to continue hunting. However, this land may be privately owned by an individual who may not want them hunting on their land. This has caused private landowners and hunters to butt heads several times in many years. Hunting is a deeply cultural aspect of many Americans' lives. With more and more land becoming privately owned, it is getting more difficult to find places to hunt an individual who doesn't own that.

Don't feel disheartened by this, as there are many ways to get around this little hiccup. First, if you are planning to hunt in an area that may see you going onto private property, all you need to do is to find out if it is posted or not.

If the property is posted—where a warning has been placed to say no trespassing or hunting is allowed—you can simply ask the owner for permission to have access to the land. It is generally good manners to do this several days before your hunt happens and not do it while hunting. Unless the owner has a sanctuary on their property or they don't want animals killed there, there is a good chance that you may be allowed to hunt on the property. Some owners may even strike a deal with you where you can pay to hunt on their property or they may want a share of your harvest. However, if an owner says no, you do not have access to the land and can be arrested for trespassing if caught on the property. Be sure to get confirmation of permission in writing just to be sure.

If an owner has refused your entrance to his property, there are only two reasons that you may go onto their land. The first is that you have wounded prey that has crossed the border or your hunting dogs have run onto the property. You must make sure both are retrieved and contact the owner to make them aware of your intent and reason for being on their property.

If privately owned land has been correctly posted, it will be clear for all to see. Each state/province has its own set of rules for how posting should be done, but the general rule for you as a hunter is to look out for several things. The first is several signs that state no entry. These can generally be found at vehicle entrances, corners of the property, and sometimes spaced out along a fence every quarter mile or so. These signs need to be legible and visible to any who may stumble across them. These signs may also be painted in bright colors such as orange or yellow to draw attention.

Sometimes the posting is not obvious, so if you are hunting and come across livestock, buildings, or cultivated land, you are in an area that you should not be. An owner may even ask you to leave, in which case it is something you need to do whether the land is posted or not. As a hunter, you need to make sure you do not enter private property. If you see a posting and ignore it, you are now hunting illegally and are, therefore, a poacher. If caught, you will lose your hunting license.

The postings are not only for your benefit but also for those on the property. Suppose the landowner is aware that there is a hunter on his land. In that case, he is likely to ensure that his livestock isn't in an area where they can get shot and ensure that other people on his property are wearing bright clothes that prevent accidental or fatal shootings. Even traps left by poachers are dangerous to the landowner, people, or animals of the property.

Luckily, many states/provinces are approaching private landowners to convince them to allow hunters onto their land. These states/provinces generally help cover possible losses or damages that may be sustained due to negligent hunters or aid the owner with extra labor or monetary rewards. Hunting is, after all, a national pastime and should be protected as much as possible. Be a responsible hunter: Ask permission to be in a privately owned place, and never enter a property where you have been denied access.

CHAPTER 2

PRACTICAL SURVIVAL EQUIPMENT AND GEAR

Now that all the paperwork has been obtained, it is time to make sure your gear and attire are ready. It isn't as simple as falling into a camping store and getting everything in one go. It will take time and some research to find the brands and items that you may prefer over another. Use the following information to do your research on what you may need personally when hunting, as some tools may not suit the type of hunt you are planning. Once you have an idea of what is perfect for you, put a shopping list together and get what is on it. Then, when you are ready to get everything gathered for your hunt—a few days before departing—have a checklist prepared to make sure that you do not forget anything. Preparation for a hunt is what takes the longest time, so spend some time setting up an appropriate checklist not to forget anything. Remember, there are no stores out in the wilderness. Once you are there and find yourself in need of something, you will have to make do without or develop creative ways to get around the problem.

HUNTING GEAR

You can get several items for yourself, but you have to decide what kind of hunt you will be going on before you get distracted by all the nifty tools. Knowing what sort of hunt you want to be a part of will determine what tools you will need. You will have no use for a pelvis saw if you are hunting rabbits. For the sake of this book, it is the smaller game animals that will be concentrated on, and even then, various tools are needed for different animals.

The first necessary thing is a decent backpack that is suited for your frame and strength. It needs to be not only sturdy enough to carry everything you may need but also manageable. You will be hiking for some distance after your quarry, so if your pack is too heavy when you start, imagine how heavy it will be when you come back with any potential prizes. The size of the backpack is determined by how long you want to be out hunting, so be sure to pack responsibly.

A skill you may need to brush up on is reading a map and using a compass. You can plan your hunting route on a map and become familiar with possible landmarks as a way to encourage yourself to not only rely on a global positioning system (GPS). This is not to say that you cannot use a GPS, but you will need to have a backup if the system fails. If you plan to use a GPS, then ensure that you have tested it well before going on your trip. Make sure the batteries it uses are fully charged, and you have spares for it. You can even make use of power banks to aid you in this. However, keep in mind that all of this does add to the weight you will have to carry with you. Many places where you can hunt may not have a decent signal, so ensure that the maps you are planning on using can be used in airplane or offline mode. OnX is one of the GPS map apps that many hunters and wardens trust to get around while searching for their specific quarry. Be responsible for plotting where you are going and informing people of when you are leaving, where you are going, and for how long. These three important aspects can mean the difference between finding you if you get lost or remaining lost in the wilderness forever.

Other possible electronics that you can make use of are handheld torches or headlamps. Although a headlamp allows your hands to be free if you are moving around or carrying something, both are great tools to have. If you are hunting in a group—with a mentor or friends—you can also use two-way radios for communication. Ensure that you have the correct batteries for all the electronics you are carrying or all the wires necessary for charging the items from power banks. If you are hunting in a group and want to scout ahead, make sure that you have some kind of trail-marking tape to mark your route to find your way back or others can find you. There is nothing quite as scary as getting lost. If this happens to you—and this is possible—the first thing you have to do is not panic. The rest of the survival tips will be covered in Chapter 3.

When one is hunting for prey, you will primarily be using your eyes. You can pick up where an animal has gone by disturbed brush, fur left on trees, or tracks and scat, but sometimes, you may want to look a little further than what is just under your nose. A good set of binoculars will help you look for prey either in the sky, trees, or among the brush. Do not skimp on quality binoculars. Some animals are easier to hunt when you use a specific call to attract them. If you know what animal you are after, and you know the call they make, then you can make use of animal calls or even prerecorded sounds to take with you. This is not a must for all animals, so make sure your quarry needs this before just taking it along.

You will need a knife and a good one at that. Whether you find yourself having to dress your kill or defend yourself in the wilderness, a knife is essential. You can choose many knives, with some people preferring to use either fixed blades, folding knives, or the ever-popular multi-tool, which has several other functions. Each of these has its pros and cons, but it is up to your preference in deciding which is best to use. Regardless of what knife you are planning on using, make sure that you have a tool that can sharpen it. There is nothing more frustrating than having a dulled tool and not doing what it must to make your life easier.

Whether you are thinking of making a single-day trip or several, it is a good idea to take some sort of shelter with you. You may think it is unnecessary, but if the weather suddenly turns nasty, you will have one more tool in your arsenal that will protect you. Something as simple as a space blanket or bivy sack can keep you warm and safe until such time that the weather improves and you can keep moving. For longer days in the wilderness, you can consider other shelter methods or ways to sleep, which can even include hammocks. These shelters should be heavily dependent on the season you are hunting in, so make sure to have the appropriate equipment that goes with the season. Other items you may need if you are going to be out for a few days are cooking utensils to cook and enjoy warm meals. These can also be used to help gather water when necessary.

Paracord (parachute cord) is a must-have item whether you are hiking or hunting. From replacing a snapped bootlace to a damaged bag cord to even hoisting your food up into a tree, this item has multiple functions and should be in all hunting bags. However, it is available in many stores in various lengths; however, check the breaking strength to determine the kind of function it will have to fulfill.

Other items that could come in handy but are dependent on the animal you are hunting are blinds and decoys. Some animals will only come close to you if they see others like themselves. If you are going to make use of blinds, be sure to sit still and comfortably. Get a few cushions, but don't fall asleep.

HUNTING ATTIRE

You need to make sure that what you wear is comfortable, protective, keeps you hidden, and makes sure that you can be seen. Many people assume that you will need to wear camouflage clothes so that the animals do not see you, but this is not true for all states/provinces. Some state and province regulations insist that you wear a high visibility vest and cap—usually orange in color—when hunting. This is to prevent other hunters from accidentally shooting you as you move through the wilderness.

Depending on the season you are hunting in, you may require extra layers of clothing to protect you from the cold or rain. The inner layer (or base layer) is there to not only keep you warm but also to keep moisture away from your skin. Hunting is hard work, and you will sweat. There is nothing worse than wet socks and underwear as you are walking, so because of this, the base layer needs to be made of a synthetic material (such as polyester) which creates a wicking effect that draws water away from your skin. Although cotton seems warmer, it absorbs moisture and keeps it close to the skin, which in turn will develop hot spots and blisters if you remain in those wet clothing items.

The outer layer—such as jackets or rainwear—needs to be waterproof and puncture proof. This layer will protect you from the elements and needs to be of high-quality material. The orange vest, if you need to wear one, will go over this. Depending on what animal you are hunting for, you can make use of scent-reduced clothing. Gloves and socks need to have a wicking effect and stand a good chance of getting wet if you are moving through the brush. Consider having a few sets of dry, clean socks in your pack, as this is how you will prevent blisters from developing. When the biting insects get to be too much, you can use bug netting draped over your hat to keep them out of your face if you do not want to use insect repellent.

The most important piece of clothing you will need is a good set of worn-in boots. These are what will protect your feet and make walking vast distances bearable. Never go hunting or hiking with a new pair of boots. The blisters will drive you insane. Boots worn during the spring and summer should be the same size as your everyday shoes. In contrast, those worn in the fall and winter need to be up to a size larger to accommodate the thicker socks you will need to make use of.

VITAL EXTRAS

These tools are not limited to hunting but rather of importance to anyone who plans on going out into the wilderness. The most vital is a basic first aid kit. This is only a starter kit, though. You will need to ensure that you know how to use everything in this kit and adapt it to one that can cover all the potential problems that can occur during a hunt. A standard first aid kit purchased from a pharmacy may not have everything that is required. The longer you are out hunting, the more items you need to have in your first aid kit. There are some no-compromise necessities such as gauze pads, butterfly bandages, Band-Aids, alcohol wipes, moleskin (for blisters), tweezers, antibiotic cream, allergy ointment, antihistamine of choice, an EpiPen, if required, ibuprofen (or painkiller of choice), surgical gloves (an allergy-free type), duct tape (a lot of this), SAM splint (flexible splint), anti-diarrhea medication, a Sharpie marker, and medical tape. Duct tape can take up a lot of space, so don't hesitate to wrap it around other items such as pencils, Sharpies, or even lighters to save space. If you have any personal or chronic medication, you will also need to pack this into your kit.

For a more advanced first aid kit, consider adding the following to help with more severe wounds that can occur. A hemostatic agent (such as QuikClot) to help stop the bleeding or make it more manageable until more fully trained help can arrive. Only if you have been trained to do so can you make use of a suture kit. If you have not been trained to do so, manage the wound with Steri-Strips or butterfly bandages. You can make use of liquid stitches or super glue to manage cuts that are not too serious. Pressure dressings not only apply pressure to a wound but also keep the dressings in place. Due to this, infection is limited, and it can stem the flow of blood. Ensure that you have enough gauze rolls, tape, dressing, and cohesive wrap so that you can manage wounds that may need redressing. If you are not using a water purifier or packing enough clean water, consider purchasing some water treatment tablets. Unpurified water can bring nasty stomach issues that can leave you dehydrated and too weak, so always stick to drinking clean water. Dehydration can be easily combated with some electrolytes in either a powdered form or a fizzy tablet. These can also provide energy to help you get through some of the difficult hikes you may have to do when looking for your quarry.

A first aid kit is only as good as what you put into it. Make sure you have quality items that have not expired. Go through the contents every couple of months to ensure that everything is up to standard. Taking an introductory first aid course isn't necessary. Still, it is something that will come in handy if a disaster were to strike. Consider doing this if for no reason other than to be fully prepared.

Sunblock is necessary, even in the middle of winter, so be sure to make use of it. You can even get lip balms containing sun protection (SPF), which can protect your lips from getting sunburned. However, it isn't just the sun that you will need to protect yourself. Whining and biting insects are a bane to all who want to enjoy a pleasant hunt.

Insect repellents in the form of sprays, wipes, or ointments will protect you from their irritating bites. However, if you are concerned that this smell may cause your quarry to avoid you, you will need to ensure that the clothes you wear can cover all the areas prone to bites.

You can never assume that all your hunts will be successful, so it is crucial to pack food and water. You can use several foods, such as jerky, gummy sweets, or even prepared food such as boiled eggs and sandwiches. You can even learn to make your own pemmican (a trail food consisting of fat and powdered meat) or trail mix to help you with the energy required for a hunt. Foods that you take with you should contain about 40% carbohydrates, 30% fat, and 30% protein to cover all your body's needs. Although food and water go hand in hand, water is most vital to your survival. You can quickly get dehydrated in a matter of hours and be dead in three days if you do not have access to water. You can carry water with you, or you will need to have a purification system.

Other miscellaneous items that will benefit you is dental floss (with a sturdy needle to fix any possible tears), black bags (excellent ground cover as well as a way to get rid of your trash), a foldable shovel (to dig pit latrines if needed), toilet paper, a fire-making kit (can include matches, lighters, and flints), zip ties, game bags, fishing kit (if your license allows for fishing, or at the very least some fishing line), writing equipment (pen, pencil, and writing pad), snare wire (or picture hanger wire), and a set of dry towels.

POSSIBLE HUNTING WEAPONS

As a hunter, you are spoiled for choice when it comes to what and how you hunt. There are many small game options which can be seen in the table below. Each animal has several ways in which you can hunt them.

Small mammals	Rabbits and hares: snowshoe hare, cottontail, and jackrabbit. Squirrels: red, gray, and fox squirrels. Prairie dogs, marmots, groundhogs, and woodchucks. Foxes (furbearers or predators): gray, red, and swift foxes. Furbearers: beavers and muskrats. Furbearers or predators: weasels, ferrets, martens, fishers, wolverines, mink, badgers, and skunks. Predators: Bobcats, lynx, and coyotes.
Birds	Grouse (upland birds): sage grouse, sharp-tailed, ruffed, blue, and Franklin's. Doves (upland birds): mourning dove, pigeon, squab (young pigeon), or rock dove. Quail (upland birds): bobwhite, scaled quail, mountain, California, and Gambel's. Partridge (upland birds): gray and chukar partridge. Pheasants (upland bird). Woodcocks and Snipe (upland birds). Turkey (upland bird). Geese (waterfowl): Canadian, Brant geese, and snow. Ducks (waterfowl): mallard, pintail, American black, wood, teal, ruddy duck, and canvasback. Swans (waterfowl): tundra, trumpeter, tundra, black, and black-necked swan. Cranes (waterfowl): sandhill crane.

Reptiles & Amphibians	Frogs: American toad, Fowler's toad, bullfrog, northern gray treefrog, northern spring peeper, western chorus frog, and northern cricket frog. Turtle: snapping turtles.

Not all areas allow for snares and traps, so be sure to check regulations before deciding on using these hunting methods.

Snares and Traps

These hunting methods can be used by a hunter who wishes to keep the pelts in good condition or simply try to survive because something went wrong and they have no other option. There are several types of snares that you can make use of to catch smaller animals. These include the simple snare (placed in the middle of an animal run or over its burrow) and a twitch snare (a simple snare attached to a sapling that catches the animal and pulls it into the air). The snare has a clinch system that tightens as the animal struggles. Simple snares can be added to a squirrel pole, which squirrels use to run up into trees to catch various animals such as squirrels and martens. You can use either snare wire or picture hanging wire to make these snares.

Traps like the deadfall trap use a heavy object (usually a rock) held up with sticks and bait under it. The prey item—usually a rat, mouse, or another type of rodent—will come for the bait and disturb the trap, which will cause the rock to land on them.

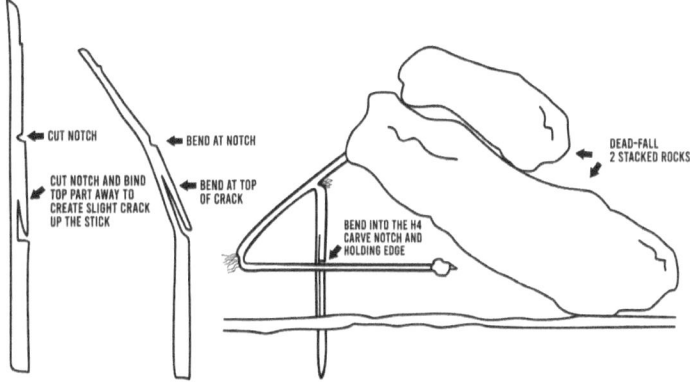

If you are looking to catch bait for fishing, you can use the bottle fish trap. When looking at a two-liter plastic soda bottle, you remove the first quarter of it—which includes the neck—and you invert it into the remaining part of the bottle. Alternatively, you can use two bottles where the head and neck section is pushed into another bottle with only a small portion of the bottom removed. Ensure that the two pieces are held together by something that can be removed later. Add to a stream, tie it in place, and wait. Small bait fish will swim into the trap but will find themselves unable to swim out again.

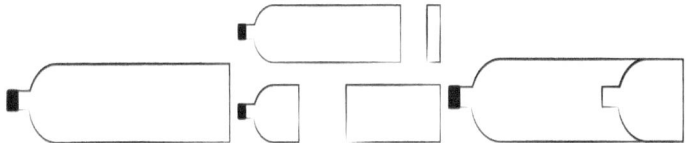

(Tip: If using two bottles, ensure that the cap at the end of the trap is in place or the fish will just swim straight out.)

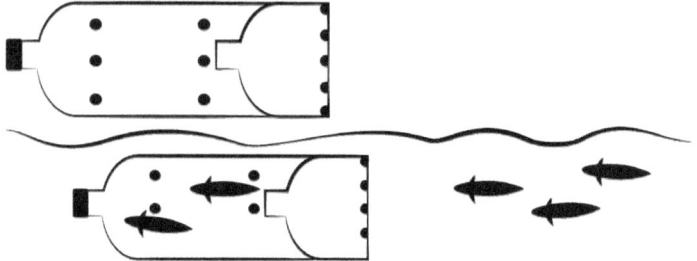

(Tip: When making use of these hunting methods, you must check the traps regularly. Not only to collect what you catch but also to dispatch any animal humanely or to prevent any predator from making off with a meal source that may be vital for your survival.)

Slingshots

Although not legal in several states/provinces, this tool can be made or bought—depending on your preference—and can be used to hunt several small game animals or varmints. Treat a slingshot the same way you would a gun, as it too can cause considerable damage in an untrained hand. Make sure to have eye protection to ensure your safety. The key to making a slingshot work in your favor is two things: the correct ammo and the correct prey.

When looking at potential ammo, do not use something that can break upon impact and cause shards to ricochet straight back at you. Using ball bearings or smooth stones is your best bet in place of marbles. The animals you can stalk with a sling include rabbits, pheasants, wild turkeys, other fowl, squirrels, ducks, and pigeons. It is key that you get within a short range so that you get a headshot off. One shot, one kill! The key to hunting is to ensure you kill humanely. As you will need to get close to your chosen prey, you will need to learn how to stalk, so make sure that your chosen ammo doesn't make any sounds while you move around, alerting your potential prey to your whereabouts.

Making a Slingshot

Making your slingshot is as easy as going outside and looking for the right branch. You are looking for a forked branch (Y-shaped) where each of the forks is roughly the same diameter. Cut the slingshot to your preferred size using a saw. If you are not in a survival situation, you can dry your branch using the microwave. Before you do this, ensure that you have weighed the wood, as this will be your indication of moisture loss. Do not take off the bark, as this could cause the wood to crack. Microwave the wood at one-minute intervals while flipping the piece of wood each time to ensure equal water loss. The wood should be losing weight per minute. Depending on what kind of tree you cut this from will determine the moisture content. The drying process is complete when the piece of wood no longer loses weight.

Watch this process closely as you do not want the wood to start charring or smoking. Once dry, cut notches about half an inch from the top of each of the forks, making sure they are the same length on each fork. You will need to get some power bands that can be store-bought ones for slingshots, or you can use the inner tube of a tire. Make sure the lengths are the same.

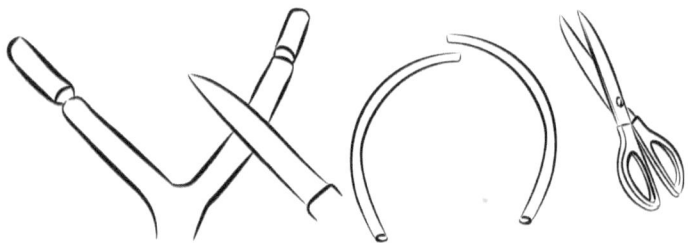

Next, lash the one open end of the powerband to the one notch using string or dental floss. You can make use of the constrictor knot or any other knot that prevents slippage. Repeat for the other fork. Take a piece of leather or other strong material that is handy, and fashion the pouch that your ammo will rest in. Make two slits in the material as you will need to attach the power bands.

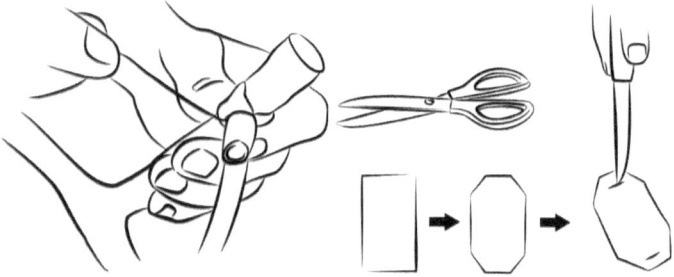

Push the power bands through the slits and tie them back onto themselves with a knot that will not slip or unravel through use.

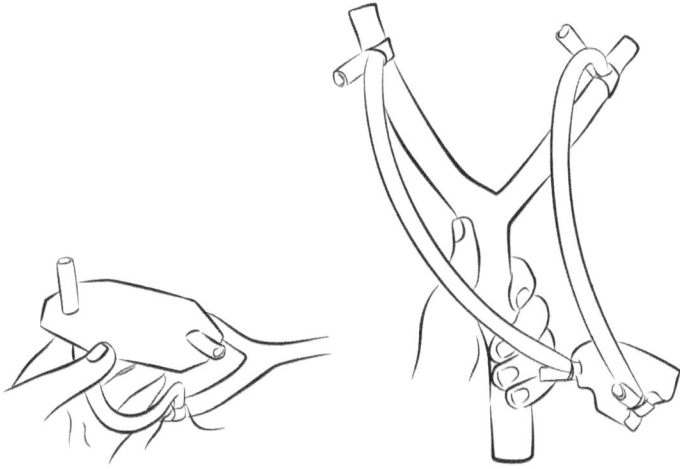

Now you have a working slingshot that will not warp as you use it because you have dried it. Try to avoid air drying, as this can cause the wood to crack, especially if you have removed the bark beforehand.

Pellet Guns

These types of guns are a step before true firearms which are just as deadly, so treat them as if they were the real thing. These weapons shoot metallic projectiles that can either be metal ball bearings (B.B.) or non-spherical pellets. Unlike firearms powered by gunpowder, these weapons can be powered by compressed CO_2 (carbon dioxide), a pump, pre-charged pneumatic (PCP), or spring charged.

This is a lightweight, easy-to-use weapon that is more accurate than most B.B. guns over a longer distance. It is also a quiet weapon, so you may have a second chance to hit your target if, for some reason, you missed the first time.

There are a variety of makes and models for pellet guns. However, suppose you are planning on hunting with this weapon. In that case, it is a good idea to use the rifle variety over the handgun type. This weapon can be used to hunt animals such as rabbits, birds, squirrels, and mice.

Not only should these weapons be treated with the same reverence as a powerful firearm but it also needs to be cleaned like one. The barrel needs to be cleaned after a hunt and obstructions removed when a misfire happens. Teach yourself how to take your weapon apart, clean it, and put it back together. If you treat your tools with respect, they will always be in top working order. Also, consider wearing eye protection when using pellet guns due to possible ricochets.

.410 Bore

This is the smallest caliber of the shotguns you can make use of for hunting. With next to no kick and cheap to reload, if you want to learn to shoot with a shotgun, this a great place to start. It is a good weapon at close range (25 yards). However, there isn't much shot per shell, so this does limit you on what you can hunt.

Some people say they have hunted many animals with this weapon. It is generally the kind of tool that is used for hunting turkeys. This shotgun is perfect for someone who is of a smaller size or very young. You may need to use a larger gauge shotgun to hunt animals such as rabbits, doves, or other game birds. That is not to say that you can't use this weapon, but rather that you will need to learn how to stalk your prey and take shots from a significantly closer range than most other firearms.

.22 Long Rifle (.22 LR)

This is an excellent firearm that doesn't have much recoil, noise, or even muzzle flash. It is a reliable tool that is lightweight enough to use while crossing long distances after prey. It is easy to fire either from a standing or prone position. Although this weapon shoots a smaller round than most other hunting weapons, it can be just as powerful and accurate in the right hands.

Unlike most hunting ammunition, the .22 is a rimfire which makes for cheaper ammunition. Still, you will not reload the ammunition as you would with most of the centerfire ammunition. However, at a fifth of the price of most 9mm rounds, it is worth it. The .22 LR comes in a variety of forms such as bolt action, pump action, semi-automatic, as well as lever action, so you can shop around for which you prefer to use. This well-rounded weapon is used for small game hunting, varmint control, target shooting, and survival.

As rimfire ammunition tends to be smaller than centerfire ammunition, there is less damage to the meat of your prey when it is shot. There are many animals you can hunt with this type of weapon. This includes smaller animals such as rabbits, squirrels, prairie dogs, and larger animals such as small deer, foxes, and wild hogs. The larger animals must be shot within a short to medium range (20–50 meters/21–54 yards), and always aim for the head or neck to ensure a quick, clean kill.

Regardless of what and where you are hunting, the only way to ensure that your trip is a success is to make sure that you are as fully prepared as possible. Expecting the worst and being prepared for it means you can handle whatever situation can be thrown at you. This chapter is but a guide. It is strongly suggested that you continue to do your research and prepare yourself fully.

CHAPTER 3

HOW TO SURVIVE—WHAT EVERY HUNTER MUST KNOW

Having the tools ready for an emergency is one thing, but knowing how to use them correctly can mean the difference between a few miserable days in the wilderness while help is on the way or something far worse. You are out there alone—or maybe with a couple of people; if something goes wrong and help is too far away, you will need to know how to protect yourself and anyone with you. Although there are several ways you can try to prepare yourself—such as checking the weather, going on first aid courses, and so on—sometimes something unexpected can occur. It is during this time that a true hunter will rise to the challenge.

GETTING LOST

When leaving civilization, there is always a chance that you can get lost. There are no roads or signs the farther you travel into the wilderness. This is why you must be familiar with the land you are traveling to, having both scoped it on a map as well as your GPS. However, even the best-laid plans can go awry. You can miss the path, slip and fall, miss a turn, and now you are hopelessly lost. The first thing you need to do is not to panic. Getting lost can be seen as a badge of honor and may have to be overcome sooner than later. When was the last time you checked your map? Can you backtrack? If so, go ahead and do this for a few minutes. If after 10 minutes nothing seems familiar, then stop and reassess the situation.

If you have some kind of communication device with a signal, then use it to call for help with the exact coordinates from your GPS. Rather, be a little embarrassed at having to be rescued than spending a night out in the wilderness. If you are with a group of people, simply calling them to alert them about where you are is the best thing you can do. This may chase your prey away, but it will ensure that you are found. You can continue to do this every couple of minutes. If, after 10 minutes, no one has come to your rescue, then your survival is up to you. Remember that well-packed backpack of yours? Well, it is what will keep you safe until such time that you can be rescued. Don't be brave and tough it out trying to walk in a random direction because you are sure civilization is in that direction. Instead, take the time to prepare several lifesaving methods—especially if the weather has turned bad—instead of losing that time and end up being more lost and unprepared.

NOW WHAT?

The first thing that you will need to do is to fight your feelings. Being lost in the wilderness is not something we are prepared for in life. Imagination can be both a wonderful and deadly thing when you are in this mindset. Some people may imagine that this is where they die while others start to hatch a plan. This is what separates a true survivor from someone that may not make it. You came prepared for this possibility, so you only need to sit and think about how you will survive. Take stock of what kinds of resources are at your disposal in your immediate vicinity, as well as what remains in your pack. Do not go wandering farther from your current situation! If you got injured while getting lost, now is a good time to go over your injuries and treat them as best as possible. Once you have assessed that you can still move around, now is the time to build a shelter.

Shelter

A human can last up to three days without water. Still, he can die within a few hours due to hyperthermia (overheating) or hypothermia (too cold). You either need to get warm or cool down as quickly as possible. The shelter doesn't need to be a log cabin. Keep it small and easy to insulate if the weather is cold, or open and ventilated if hot. Even if you have a bivy sack or a space blanket, a simple shelter is enough to keep most of the elements at bay and points to the fact that a human is in the vicinity. This will help other people to find you.

Regardless of whether you are building a simple or a fully protected shelter, you will need to start with a sturdy frame, or you may find that the structure meant to keep you safe collapses around you. When in a forest, see if you can spot two saplings or small trees about six to seven feet apart. If this isn't something you see around you, but there are sparse trees, you can cut down a sapling then bring it closer to another tree. Dig a 12-inch hole to bury this sapling. These two standing trees or saplings will be the start of your frame. Find another sapling or thick branch that you can tie vertically between these two standing saplings—this will be your weight-bearing support beam—and tie it at the height of choice. Tie it higher for cooling down and lower for insulating your heat. Alternatively, suppose a tree nearby has some low-hanging branches that are sturdy. In that case, you can stake one into the ground, and it can be both the support beam and secondary part of the frame.

Ensure that your support beam isn't rotten and can take some weight. Once the frame is sturdy, you can add up to five layers of thick branches angled from the ground to your support beam. By placing these branches at an angle, it will help with keeping the rain off of you. You can use longer branches for a shelter against heat and shorter for a refuge against the cold. Cut these branches from trees where necessary and ensure that no insects or animals can bite you while you work. Depending on the situation you find yourself in, you can decide to build two walls—which can give the appearance of a tent—or a single wall which is the traditional shelter. Continue to pack on these branches until the entire length of your shelter is covered.

Once the angled roof is complete, the next step is to start waterproofing and insulating it. Collect small branches with leaves and pack them along the wall, first running horizontally and vertically until the layer is about a foot thick. If you still find gaps, you can fill those with more leaves, smaller sticks, bark, moss, and even pine needles. If you sit or lie in the shelter, you should not see outside through the wall. Now you know that it is truly well insulated.

The next step is the floor of your shelter. Suppose you are trying to protect yourself from the heat. In that case, you need to clear the spot of debris and dig down into the ground, which will be significantly cooler than the air around you. Keep yourself from dehydrating and wait to do anything further until it is cooler not to waste any of your precious water. Suppose you need to protect yourself from the cold. In that case, you will also have to clear the area of debris before laying down an insulating layer, as the ground will be cold.

The same material you used to insulate your shelter's walls is good enough for your ground cover. If you have a groundsheet or black bags, you can lay this down over the insulating layer to give you more protection. You can even cover the entrance with this insulating material to keep the warmth in your small shelter.

(Tip: There are several ways to build a shelter—as is seen in the images. Which one you decide to build comes down to the materials that you find in your proximity and equipment you have with you.)

Water

Once your shelter is complete, you need to work on finding a fresh source of clean water to keep you going. If there is a storm or it is too hot, it is best to remain in your shelter and do what you have until the dangerous weather has passed. Once it is safe to do so, you can scope the area around you to find moving water. Ensure that you are marking your trail, as you do not want to get separated from your only shelter. If you cannot locate fresh, moving nearby water, look around you to see if there are any catchment areas where water may pool naturally. This water is likely stagnant, but it is worth collecting and storing until such time that you can boil it to make it safe. If there is snow nearby, you can collect that, but do not eat the snow directly! It takes a lot of energy to warm your body, and you will just lower it to the point of hypothermia if you are going to eat snow constantly. Instead, collect it and melt it down.

If you are uninjured, you can also dig for water. Look for plants known to grow close to water sources, such as cattails, willows, or cottonwood (Dumbauld, 2019). Dig a hole close to this plant until you notice moisture in the soil. Dig a little deeper and widen the hole. You have just created a weep hole that will naturally collect the water rising from the ground.

You can also collect water from plants directly because of the dew that lands on them. Be careful when taking water from plants directly without knowing what kind of plant it is. Some plants contain toxic components that can make your bad situation even worse. Only drink from plants that you recognize as safe. You can also tie plastic bags—such as Ziploc bags—around clusters of leaves, as when the plant goes through its respiration cycle, a by-product is water. Lastly, you can simply leave a piece of cloth or towel out to collect dew which can then be squeezed out and collected. Always ensure that you have some sort of container with you when hunting to collect water in it.

Many of these water-catching techniques are not quick. They will take some time to give you more than just a few mouthfuls of this lifesaving liquid, so be sure to have as many different types of catchments and learn to ration as much as possible without getting dehydrated.

Fire

You can never assume that the water you collect is clean, so it is always a good idea to boil it for a few minutes to get rid of any kind of pathogens that can lead to an upset stomach. Fire is essential not only because it can keep your water supply clean, but it can also keep you warm, cook any meals you manage to catch, and protect you from possible predators. A warm, full belly makes any situation a lot easier to deal with.

Starting a fire may be simple enough, but keeping it alive and going is something that takes a little more preparation and planning. You should already have the tools to help you create the fire, so move to the preparation for what else you may need. The success of any fire is keeping it fueled from birth until your rescue, so set out to find tinder, kindling, and fuelwood (thick sticks or branches). If you have a fire starting kit in your pack, there may already be tinder ready for you to use, but if not, create your own by collecting dried leaves, grass, finger-length twigs, or even pine needles. These items need to be dry to catch fire. Collect enough to create a bundle that can be held between your two hands with fingers touching. Next, collect some kindling. Kindling can be small sticks that should be no thicker than your index finger. You will need to collect about a generous armful. After that, it is time to look for fuelwood. This wood is about the thickness of your wrist, the length of your arm, and you need to collect enough that the stack comes to just under your knee.

Once everything has been collected, you can also look for some stones to help protect your fire and create a firepit. Whether you are trying to survive or not, this is not the time to forget that it is very dangerous when a fire isn't controlled. You need to clear debris away from where you want to build your fire. The distance from your shelter to your fire will be determined by the type of weather you are exposed to. Once the debris has been removed, you can dig down a little into the ground to create your firepit. Stones can also surround this firepit to help protect it from the wind while trying to light the tinder.

Build a small teepee with your kindling in the firepit first. Then take your tinder and create a nest into which you add a lit match, light a tinder bundle with a lighter, or make some scrapings from a magnesium block and lighting it with a striker. Add the lit tinder to the teepee of kindling and gently blow on the bundle until the flame starts to consume it and starts on the kindling. Continue to add more kindling until the fire begins to grow in strength. Once the kindling pile starts to diminish, then add the fuelwood around it. You can stack it around the fire or create another teepee over it. Now you have a fire.

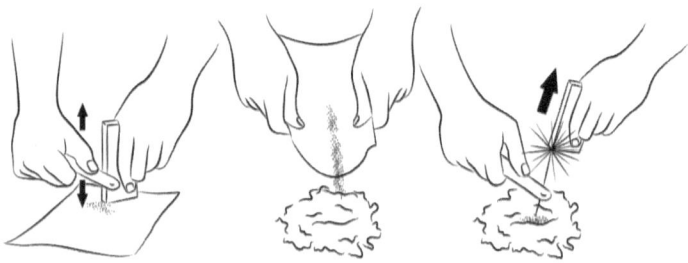

(Tip: Do not breathe in close to the smoking tinder as you will get a lung full of smoke that is dangerous. Breathe away from it, then gently blow out over it.)

If it is freezing, you can add stones to the fire, allowing them to heat up before burying them under a layer of dirt and insulation at the bottom of your shelter to help you remain warm during the night. This is a surefire way to create smokeless heat within your shelter. Be careful not to burn yourself while trying this. Aim to pick up the hot rocks with a Y-shaped stick so that you do not touch them directly.

What happens if you lose your fire-making equipment? Well, then you need to learn how to make a bow drill. As long as you have a knife or multi-tool, paracord or rope, and wood, you can make this ancient tool to give you fire. You will need a flat piece of medium to hard type wood (this will be your fireboard or hearth board) with a socket in it—you can cut it into the wood—and a spindle made of the same wood. The fire board should be between ½ to ¾ inch thick and at least twice as wide as your spindle. The spindle needs to be made with a straight piece of wood with a diameter of ¾ of an inch with a length of about 8-12 inches, preferably round in shape. The top end must taper off to a blunted point, while the bottom should also taper but not as sharply. This will go into the fireboard. These two pieces of wood must be dry!

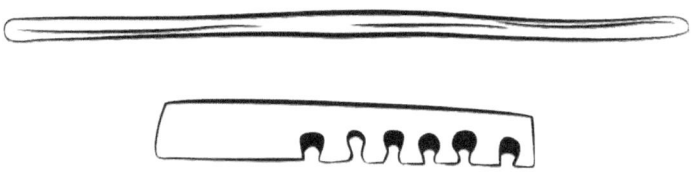

Next, you will need to make your handhold and your bow. The handhold will be placed on top of the spindle to hold it in place, creating a notch for where this point will be, and bore some wood out. You will need to grease this area, as you do not want it to smoke while making an ember. The bow needs to be about the length of your forearm, slightly curved, and have a little flexibility to it. You will tie the paracord to both ends to create a bow with little slack in the cord. Take the spindle, ensuring that it has no bark still attached to it, and set it against the cord, making sure that it is in the center of the spindle. Twist the top of the spindle to the bottom, wrapping the cord around it. The cord should loop around the spindle—keeping it in place—with the bow on one side. The spindle should be on the outer edge of the cord and not between it and the bow. Do not let the cord rub against itself. The best way to achieve this is to angle the bow slightly downward when you are using it.

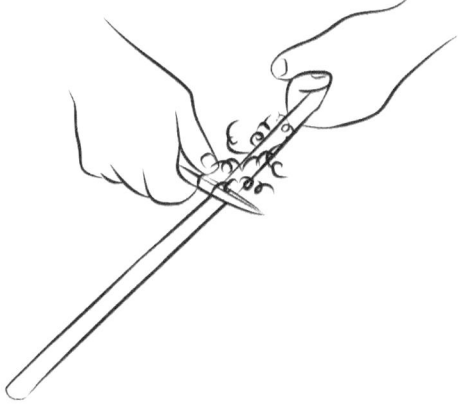

Set the broader tapered end of the spindle into the socket in the fireboard while holding it steady with your handhold on top. Now, move the bow back and forth at a steady pace until you see smoke starting to form. If the spindle hasn't jumped from the socket, then it is deep enough. If it has jumped from the socket, then go ahead and make it deeper. This is the drilling step and will ensure nothing jumps out of place when creating an ember. The fireboard must not move, so be sure to keep it in place by setting one of your feet on it.

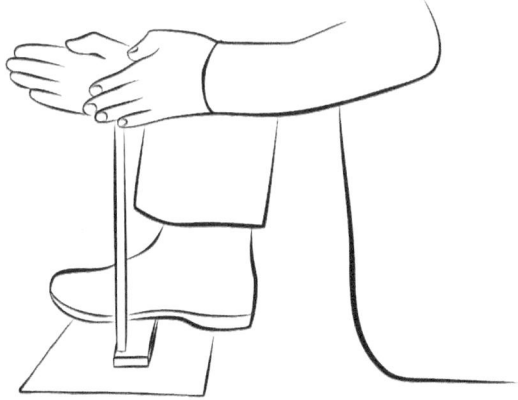

The next step is to cut a notch in the lower socket, about an eighth of the socket; this will allow the coal dust to fall on a waiting piece of bark or green leaf, igniting into an ember. This notch is to provide oxygen without the spindle leaving the socket. Ensure that all the burning materials are ready before you start. Set everything up again and move the bow back and forth to create the black dust that will birth a burning ember. As you move the bow and spindle, you will notice that smoke is rising. Lift the spindle to see if you have coal by fanning the black dust to see if it turns red. Suppose it does, then transfer it to your tinder nest. Once on the tinder, you can gently blow on it until you notice flames. Then follow the steps with the kindling until you have a fire. It may take some practice to get this right, so practice this skill before going hunting.

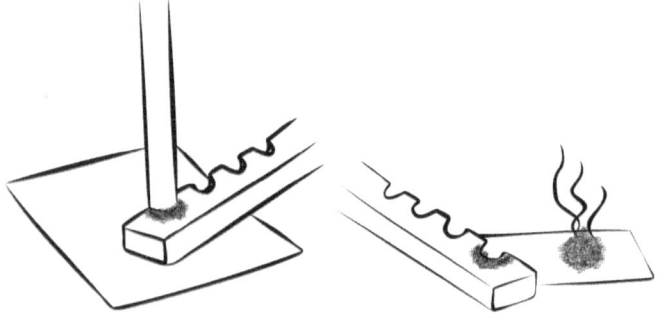

If you do not have a cord, you will have to make one with your shoelace or forgo the bow drill and just use the hand drill. This is where you use your hands to twist the spindle back and forth while applying pressure rather than the bow doing the work. You may need a thinner and longer spindle to achieve this by hand.

If you are injured or too exhausted, there is an easier way to make a fire if you have a cell phone with a removable battery or any other type of battery and some tinfoil. To make sure you have spare tinfoil, make sure to have some chocolate in your pack or keep some in your fire starting kit.

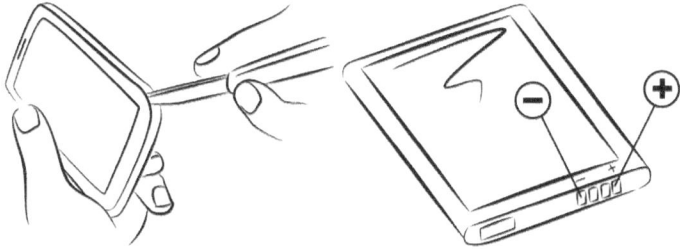

Once you have removed the battery from the phone, identify the positive and negative parts. These are marked on the battery, so it should be easy to note. Take your tinfoil and roll or fold it to create two prongs with a loop in the center. Halfway between the prongs and loop, make a bend, as this is where the tin foil will contact the battery.

(Tip: This will be fast and hot, so protect your fingers and make sure that you have your tinder ready to catch fire.)

Apply the bend in the tinfoil to the battery and set it close to your tinder. Depending on how thick you rolled your tinfoil, it may take a few seconds before you notice the smoke coming from the tinfoil. The charge from the battery causes the tinfoil to heat up and smoke before it eventually bursts into flame. Avoid damaging the battery if your phone is still functional.

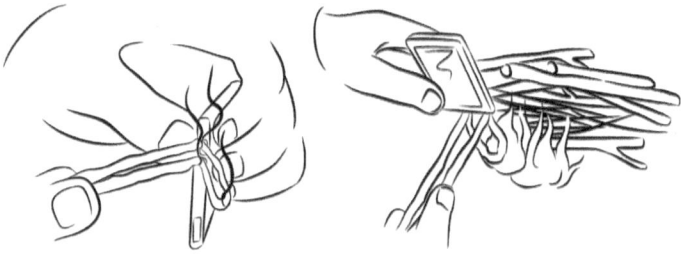

Food

The only thing missing now is the steady supply of food you require to keep your energy up as you wait for help. Your supplies will not last forever, but if it is dried, it is best to keep that for a later time when you cannot hunt or if you failed to bag something. You still have your weapon of choice, so you can still harvest food. However, ammunition does run out, and you may find that you have to rely on a backup hunting tool to still gather the food you need.

A weapon that allows you to have some distance between you and your prey is the spear. A spear can be made simply by carving a long, sturdy stick down to a point, but this is not the only way. You can also split the point to create a fork, and you can strengthen this fork by tying a wooden wedge or stone to keep the fork open. To create a three-pronged spear, you can add a third sharpened stick to this and tie it in place. This can hunt several small animals you can sneak up on or barb the ends to create a fishing spear.

Hunting isn't your only means of getting a fresh food source in your general vicinity. Suppose you have taken any wildlife courses that allow you to identify different trees, plants, and mushrooms. In that case, you can also try your hand at gathering from these food sources to keep yourself going. However, if you are not familiar with a species, do not eat it at all! Some of the edible mushrooms include the morel mushrooms (which have a honeycomb-like cap), the hedgehog mushroom (also known as the sweet tooth or wood hedgehog, which have a smooth top cap but a spiky bottom), the black trumpet mushroom (which looks like a small, black trumpet), and hen-of-the-woods (also known as ram's or sheep's head, or maitake, which looks like a clump of coral) (Fratt, 2018).

There are several edible plants throughout North America, and depending on when and where you hunt, you can make use of most of them. Plants such as clover, dandelions, rosehips, wild asparagus, cattails (also known as punks), and even green seaweed or kelp are easily recognized. Most of the plants can be utilized (MacKay &

MacKay, 2020). A common rule of thumb when it comes to the safety of choosing the right plant is that you avoid anything that has a milky or discolored sap, contains spines or fine hairs, or has a bitter taste. Similarly, with mushrooms, if you cannot identify the plant with 100% accuracy, give it a complete skip. Even if you see an animal eating it, don't assume the same can be said for you eating it.

Something else that you shouldn't turn your nose up at is eating insects. As long as it isn't brightly colored, has a sting, or covered in hair, it is edible. Crickets, grasshoppers, and termites are a great source of protein and can be fried so that you can enjoy a nice crunch while you eat them. You can even eat earthworms and slugs or use them as bait for fish if you have access to a river or ocean.

> (Tip: Be sure to count the legs; if it has more than six, give it a skip.)

If you are close to the ocean, look to crustaceans like crabs or other marine life such as turtles as other food sources. You are trying to survive, and you may have to let go of beliefs such as "Ew, gross! I can't eat that!" This could be your only chance to survive until help arrives. Depending on the season, you can even look for eggs or nesting birds. Clubbing a roosting or nesting bird as it sleeps is a sure way to get a meal without having to chase an animal down. Bird bones are great to make hooks with if you plan on going fishing.

Your food isn't just about fats, proteins, and carbohydrates; it is also about vitamins and minerals. Within a few days, you can start seeing the result of missing these parts in your diet. Although you can get vitamin B from eating animals and calcium from insects or crustaceans, you cannot go wrong by making some tea with fresh pine or spruce needles to give you the necessary vitamin C (Bennett, 2016).

> (Tip: Keep your eyes open for anything that can help you. Trash like candy wrappers, old cans, and glass bottles can all help you survive a little longer by helping with making fire or catching water.)

CHAPTER 4

SMALL GAME FOR STARTERS

Most people aren't ready to hunt a black bear or even a moose on their first day out, so look into hunting small game animals until you have built up the confidence to tackle the larger animals. The satisfaction of hunting a squirrel is just as exciting as taking your first deer. Some small game animals in several states/provinces can be hunted year-round instead of limited to a short few days or weeks, as seen with several large game animals. As hunting is becoming more popular—and the cost of it is rising every year—the chance of getting a shot at bagging your particular quarry of choice is becoming rarer every hunting season, so hunting small game is a perfect way for you to hone your skills while you wait for those sought-after tags.

Several small animals—from squirrel size to turkey size—will be discussed in better depth in this section. These animals are likely in your backyard—please don't hunt in your backyard unless you are well away from civilization—and rarely require tags. However, check your state or provincial requirements for various licenses before picking up your hunting weapon of choice and heading out to find them. Each state/province also has its unique hunting season per particular animal, as well as how many you are allowed to hunt per day (bagging) or have on your person (holding), so be sure to brush up on this knowledge.

SQUIRREL

There are several squirrel species that you can hunt for several months of the year—usually between September and January. The bagging limit per species per day is generally between four and six. Squirrels are arboreal (tree-living) rodents with large bushy tails that come in various colors that vary from gray, black, brown, and even red. Their diet consists mainly of tree nuts, seeds, tree buds, berries, fungi (mushrooms), and even crops if they are in the area.

Squirrels are preyed upon by many different birds, reptiles, and predators. They tend only to live a few years in the wild. The areas you are likely to find squirrels—in most parts of America and Canada—are mixed forests that contain the food source they need to survive. They also like to nest, and that is one way that you can track them. Their nests are similar to that of crows but messier and contain more leaves. These animals tend to have between one and two litters a year that contain anywhere from two to four kits/pups (baby squirrels) safely cared for by the female. The gestation period (pregnancy) is about 45 days, and the kits/pups are born during the latter part of spring into summer.

Another way to track that a squirrel has been through an area is to create divots in the ground and snow looking for their cache of stored food. Although squirrels are known for hiding their food, they do not always remember where it was hidden and are likely to use another squirrel's cache as much as their own.

Squirrels can be hunted in three ways: spot-and-stalk, stop-and-go hunting, and ambush hunting. The best time to hunt them is in the morning—not too early as they do not like the cold—and evenings. As a beginner, an excellent way to start hunting them is to simply sit at the base of a tree and wait, listening for their movements. They are not known to be quiet as they run through the trees. Squirrel is quite edible and has dark meat that tastes similar to chicken but is somewhat tougher yet full of flavor. You can drop this prey with either a .22 rifle—aim for the head—or a shotgun with #6 pellets. If you are confident, you can try a slingshot if the squirrel is on the ground. Learning to hunt squirrels will sharpen your skills in stalking and patience while you get to enjoy the beautiful view.

RABBIT

Rabbit season includes rabbits and hares. The two animals are vastly different, but the easiest way to remember the difference is that a hare is born above ground, fully furred, and ready to run. Meanwhile, a rabbit is born underground in a warren, naked, blind, and requires constant care from its mother.

Depending on which state or province you find yourself in, hares and rabbits may be hunted year-round, while other species of rabbits, you can only hunt during the fall and winter. Unlike pet rabbits, the wild varieties tend to be dull browns and grays, while the cottontails have a white underbelly and under tail with rust-colored fur around the neck. Generally, hunting licenses for these animals are affordable. It is very much worth it, as this meat is worth the hunt. Cottontail especially is excellent, as it can be treated the same way as chicken yet manages to have its unique flavor.

Their diet consists of most things vegetative, but they will resort to eating bark during the winter. They have several predators that hunt them, including animals such as mink, bobcats, and birds of prey that fly by night and day. If a predator can chase the rabbit, it gets to eat it. The standard life span is less than four years, but a female can have up to five litters a year with as many as nine kittens. Both rabbits and hares prefer thick grass or brush so that they can hide.

However, those from the western parts of the U.S.A. find shelter more often in rocky outcrops.

Signs of passing are generally the running trails and dropping these animals leave behind, but you can also note where the bark has been chewed off of trees. If checking the brush, look for plant stems that have been eaten, as they tend to have a very sharp angle due to the teeth of these animals.

Primarily, these creatures are nocturnal due to the number of predators that eat them, and they will avoid open areas where possible. The best time to hunt rabbits is in the morning and evenings where they will be lounging around the entrance of their warrens. There are several ways to hunt rabbits. If the state/province allows it, you can use snares over the entrance of the warren or in their trail runs. Generally, the spot-and-stalk method is best, and you will only get a single chance to shoot, as they are jumpy animals and will run for their warrens if spooked. Rifles and shotguns can be used.

GROUSE

A grouse is a type of pheasant that comes in various colors, including brown, gray (found in colder places), red (found in warmer areas), and even white. Hunting season on these birds is between September and December, and the bag limit may depend on which grouse you want to hunt. A grouse can easily be identified separately from a partridge. They tend to have small feathers in their nostrils and their legs covered up with feathers until their toes.

Many species are found in both forests and mountains and are a prize for any hunter's plate. While Spruce and Greater-Sage Grouse tend to taste like the plants they eat—and their namesake—the Ruffed Grouse has sweet white meat similar to lean chicken, while the Sharp-tailed Grouse and Rock Ptarmigan tend to have dark meat that is gamey and similar to duck. With that being said, pick your flavor and go hunting for it.

The diet of these birds varies from catkins, buds, twigs, soft fruits, ferns, acorns, and even insects. Reptiles, birds, and mammals feed on the adult grouse as easily as they do the juveniles and eggs. A female grouse can lay anywhere from eight to 14 buff-colored eggs, which can take up to two days to lay a clutch. It takes up to 26 days to incubate all the eggs. The hatchlings can immediately start foraging for food and can fly within five days. Nests are generally made up of depressed leaves close to cover so the female can watch for predators.

These birds may have to be flushed from hiding so you can make use of dogs to aid in this, or you can walk around trying to find them yourself. A smaller gauge shotgun is perfect for hunting these tiny birds. You will know you are in grouse territory because the males drum their wings to attract females. You will need to keep an eye out to find them.

PARTRIDGE

Although a little smaller than most grouse, the partridge family boasts far more colors, especially the males. The barring recognizes these birds on their legs and the gorget (black mask) over their eyes. Their legs are featherless and, depending on the species, can either be bright red or orange. These birds like the open areas such as farmlands and grassy fields, so spotting them is quite possible while walking.

When hunting with dogs, these birds tend to flush downhill then run uphill, so look out for that if you are hunting with a dog. You will have to do quite a bit of walking to get the perfect shot. The diet of these birds consists of grains and seeds with a side of insects if available. The female will lay between 12 and 18 olive-colored eggs, which will hatch during June up until late July. Upon hatching, the chicks will start to forage on their own. Similar to the grouse, these birds are also accosted by many birds, mammals, and reptilian predators that will eat them during their life cycle.

To track these animals, look along a farm's field edge or even roadsides for them. They like to hide in sparse cover or short grass along these borders. They tend to feed out in the open during the early morning and late afternoon while spending the rest of the day wandering around. These birds are more easily hunted with a smaller gauge shotgun.

Hunting season on these birds is between September and January. Your bag limit can be anything from four to eight a day. Their meat is somewhat darker than most bird species—though the breast meat is still white—but is rather tasty with a mild flavor.

QUAIL

This is probably the smallest of the bird species that you will hunt for food. In the eastern parts of the U.S.A., these birds tend to live in grasslands and pine forests while they live in more mountainous or even desert locations in the West. Regardless of where they live, they are ground-dwelling birds. They do not have very good endurance for flying yet are excellent runners. These birds will fly up in groups if startled, so many hunters like to use dogs when seeking out this bird.

Most of the quail species tend to be dull grayish. Some can even have red, black, or white feathers mixed in. They also tend to have plumage that looks similar to scales on their chest. A female will lay between 12 and 16 eggs between April and June and take about 23 days to hatch. The food of choice for these birds is seeds, berries, any available fruit in the area, and insects. They can live up to three years in the wild.

Hunting season starts in October and ends in February—the same months vary from place to place—and the bag limit is usually up to eight. They are tasty birds with their own unique flavored white meat. The use of a .410 bore is perfect for this bird. However, note that there are protected quail as they are being endangered due to habitat loss. Ensure where and what you are hunting to give those endangered a fighting chance to get their numbers up.

DUCKS

Several duck species can be hunted all over Canada, America, and even Mexico. One of the most popular is the mallard. These birds are so sought after that they are very predictable—as some are migratory—and they have high-quality meat that many people enjoy. The coloration of ducks can vary from browns, whites, blacks, and even bright colors such as blues and greens. Generally, the males are brighter in color than their female companions. This is a good thing as most states/provinces regulate the hunting of females more than males.

Hunting season for ducks extends from September to February, and bag limits vary from location to location. As these are aquatic birds (waterfowl), you will find them at any body of water which includes but is not limited to ponds, lakes, ditches with water, and reservoirs. Ducks that do migrate do it to remain close to liquid water. Their diet consists of aquatic plants and many crops. Insects are usually only eaten during the mating season to build up protein reserves for laying eggs.

As ducks spend time on both land and water, their predators include reptiles, mammals, birds, and large fish, taking the juveniles with ease. Despite having many predators, most ducks can live up to a decade or more in the wild. Females typically lay clutches of between one and 13 eggs—at a rate of roughly one egg a day—between February and May. These eggs incubate for between 23 and 33 days.

Ducks can easily be tracked, as you can see their tracks in the mud surrounding the water and several feathers in the general vicinity. When you hunt for a duck can be heavily dependent on what role the weather plays, but generally, morning and late afternoon are good times to start your hunt. There are many ways to hunt ducks, from stalking to using duck calls and decoys. A smaller gauge shotgun is once again best to use when hunting duck, but any weapon you have a good aim with is good enough.

TURKEY

This is the largest of the birds you will hunt in America. Several species of these birds vary in dark colors with a few feathers that are bronze, green, or even copper. The necks are featherless, while the males have spurred legs, either blue or redheads, and they have a tuft of feathers on the chest called a beard. The females can also have this beard but to a lesser effect and have dull feathers. Both sexes have white-tipped rump and tail feathers.

Turkeys have excellent eyesight, so you will have to wear camouflage—with orange if the state/province requires it—and make use of stalking tactics as well as using the necessary calls to attract the birds. The habitat of these birds can vary from desert to savanna, with the birds preferring grasslands to feed and mate and forests to roost and avoid predators. Sure signs of turkey in the area include dusting bowls and scratch marks of feeding.

A turkey's diet varies from nuts, fruits, seeds, grasses, crops, insects, snails, and small rodents. They can live up to five years and are preyed upon by various nest raiders and predators such as mountain lions for the adults and owls for the younger birds. The female lays up to 12 eggs at a rate of an egg a day. Incubation only starts after the last egg is laid so that the whole clutch can be born within 28 days. Turkey season is split into a fall season—where both sexes are hunted—and a spring season, where only the male is hunted. Usually, turkey hunting is from sunrise to sunset, and you will need tags to hunt them.

The turkey can be quartered the same as a chicken and contains white breast meat, while the legs, wings, and thighs are of darker, tougher meat. You can also make use of the giblets such as the gizzard, heart, and liver if you are so inclined. There are strict laws on hunting turkey, so check your regulations before picking up a favored weapon.

BULLFROG

Bullfrogs are one of the largest frogs in the world, up to six inches in length. You will need to keep an eye on the regulations of the state/province you are in. In some, this animal is an invasive species, and you can hunt them freely, while others have a bag limit. The hunting season for bullfrogs is unique and widely different in each state/province.

The bullfrogs vary in color from brown, greenish-gray, light olive, or yellowish-green with a large external eardrum. They also have large webbed hind feet. They are omnivorous as well as cannibalistic and will not hesitate to eat other bullfrogs when hungry. They live in areas that have permanent water sources for their breeding, living, and feeding. Females lay up to 10,000 eggs that will hatch within two to five days. The tadpole usually overwinters in the mud and will transform into adult frogs when the weather starts to warm, but this can also take up to two years to complete. Even the adults overwinter in the mud. They have many predators that cover most of the animal kingdom.

These frogs are active day and night, although most people prefer to hunt them by night. They are easily traceable through their loud sounds, so a sit-and-wait tactic is best to use. They can be hunted with spears, bows, and even a gig (a type of fish spear). The best part of the frog to eat is the legs—fried, grilled, or boiled—with a taste and texture similar to chicken.

SNAPPING TURTLE

This is likely the most dangerous of the small game you will get to hunt. This large reptile (as large as 68 pounds), with its protective shell, saw-toothed scales, and long tail (longer in males than females), has a large head on a long neck with a beak that can remove fingers if you are not careful. As this animal likes to hide in weed-choked permanent wetlands in the mud, their coloration tends to vary from black to light brown. They are an opportunistic feeder that will eat anything from carrion to fresh plant matter.

They will hibernate during winter under logs or in the mud, either singularly or as a community. The female will lay between 20 and 40 eggs per clutch in gravel pits or soil banks, then she will leave. These turtles are very vulnerable on land, as they cannot pull their head or limbs into their shells. Hunting season is generally between July and March, avoiding the mating and egg-laying season.

These animals can be hunted in several ways, such as traps (if allowed in the state/province), hooks, or even nets. You will need to distract the head—get a sturdy stick—to grab the tail if you want to avoid receiving a painful bite. The animal can be quartered and cooked exactly like chicken, though its meat is a little darker in color.

LARGER PREY

As your skills grow, you may want to move onto larger prey and maybe even hunt other predators. You can hunt many species that will be discussed at length in another book, but here is a taste of what is available to you.

Deer

The season for hunting deer (between July and February) is limited by the weapon you choose to use (muzzleloader, crossbows, bows, and general guns), zones within the location, and various states or provinces. These animals are used for meat, pelts, and even trophies.

Moose

This is one of the biggest animals you will get to hunt, as it towers over 7.5 feet and weighs in at 1,800 pounds. Usually, the hunting season is from September to October. Still, some states/provinces will stop the season if there isn't a stable population of this animal. Even if there is a stable population, the tags are awarded through a lottery system.

Bear

This hunting season is from mid-October to early January. How you hunt—hounds, spot-and-stalk, or bait—the bear varies significantly from place to place. Tags are required, and you can either use a gun or a bow. Bear is edible—as it is an omnivore—but it is dependent on the location and the time of the year.

Wolf

In 2019, you could only hunt wolves as trophies in Alaska, Montana, Idaho, and Wyoming—each having its duration for the hunting season—and in other states/provinces, they were heavily protected. However, as of January 4th, 2021, the gray wolf was delisted as a protected species. The hunting season for these animals will start as of November 2021. Until such time, the only reason you are allowed to kill a wolf is if it is on your property and it is attacking you, your pets, or livestock.

CHAPTER 5

IDENTIFYING SIGNS AND TRACKS

Unless you physically see the animal you want to hunt before you, you will need to track them to find where they are. Each animal has a unique track and signs that it leaves behind as it moves through its territory. A true hunter will use what is left behind to stalk and get the quarry they are after. Similar animals leave similar signs, so be sure to use your eyes and ears to note the animal to ensure that you are hunting the correct one.

Tracking isn't just about what you see before you. You need to be sure of what is around you at all times. This is not only for your safety but also to ensure that you remain within your hunting license's specifications. You cannot hunt an animal that crosses outside of the area allowed to hunt in. You also cannot cross over into posted private property. So yes, keep an eye on the signs, and ensure that you know what is happening in your general vicinity.

AGE OF TRACKS

It is pointless to follow tracks that are days old, so you need to be sure of the age of the track before setting off in a direction. Tracks are subjected to many factors which can cause them to look newer or older. If tracks are covered by leaves or dust, think about when it was windy. If the tracks are in mud or snow, then step next to it and compare your tracks with the animal's tracks to see how different they look from each other. Sharp edges to the track mean that it is fresh. However, when tracking in snow, this can be a bit misleading due to the possibility of the top layer melting and freezing, giving it the appearance of being fresh. Compare tracks that are found in direct sunlight with those made in the shade. Those in the shade tend to be more accurate, as they would have been less exposed to being melted and refreezing.

WHEN TO TRACK

The best time to track an animal depends on where you want to shoot it. Suppose you are tracking an animal in the morning. In that case, you are likely to find it laying down to rest—depending on the species—while tracking later in the afternoon, and you could find the animal feeding. Knowing what to expect from the animal will allow you to make decisions, such as going toward a bedded area where the animal may be resting or getting ahead of the tracks to wait for the animal to reach its feeding grounds. The longer you practice your stalking techniques, the better you will become at it.

SQUIRREL

As these are tree-dwelling creatures, you can count yourself very lucky if you manage to find their tracks. The prints left behind look similar to those of rats with a longer hind foot than the forefoot. The size of the footprints is dependent on the species of squirrel you are hunting. The hind foot has five toes each, while the forefoot has four.

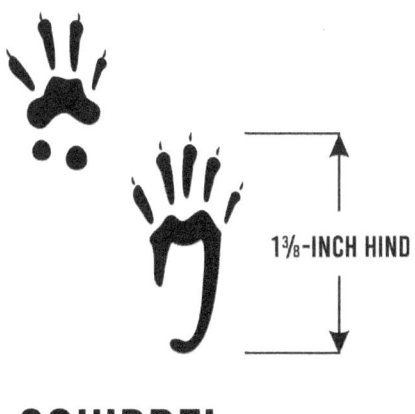

SQUIRREL

Squirrels are known as gallopers or hoppers, which means when they walk, their hind feet will move in front of their forefeet. They will also keep their feet together as they move, and you may not necessarily see the heel of their hind feet, so keep an eye on the number of toes you can count. The hind footprints will also point slightly outward. Other signs of squirrels include chewed nut husks and holes dug where they are looking for or burying their nut caches. Their droppings are easily recognizable—as though they may seem similar to rat droppings—and they are larger and barrel-shaped. They do not end in a taper like their rodent cousins. These droppings can be found at the foot of trees in little piles or singularly.

RABBIT

Rabbits, such as cottontails, have hairy feet, so it is a little more difficult to count the number of toes. However, they also have an elongated back foot—measuring 3–4 inches—and a smaller, round forefoot measuring about an inch. A jackrabbit's paws are a little bigger and have less fur on the underside of their feet, so with their tracks, you can see four toes in the front and four toes in the back.

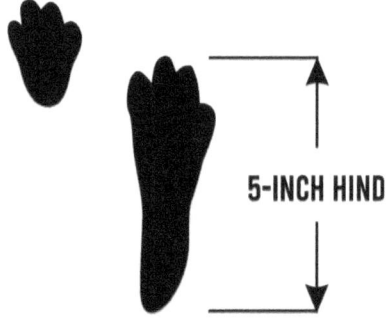

JACKRABBIT

Similar to squirrels, rabbits are also gallopers or hoppers. However, their feet tend to be more staggered than squirrels, and they do not always align with each other. The tracks of cottontails, snowshoe hares, and jackrabbits are identical in shape though sizes vary between the species. Rabbit scat can be found wherever the animal is resting or eating and are generally round, semi-dry droppings that form a small pile. Softer, darker droppings that are clumped together may be noted from time to time. Other ways to track these animals while on a hunt is with lights (spotlighting) where you note the eyeshine. However, this way of hunting may be illegal in many states/provinces, so check your regulations before attempting it. Keep an eye out for feeding damage by rabbits, such as ring barking (where a ring around the base of trees is missing bark) and plants being chewed off at a sharp angle.

UPLAND BIRDS

Upland wild game birds—these being the grouse, partridge, and quail—all have similar tracks and behaviors. However, their size, shape, and coloration may be different.

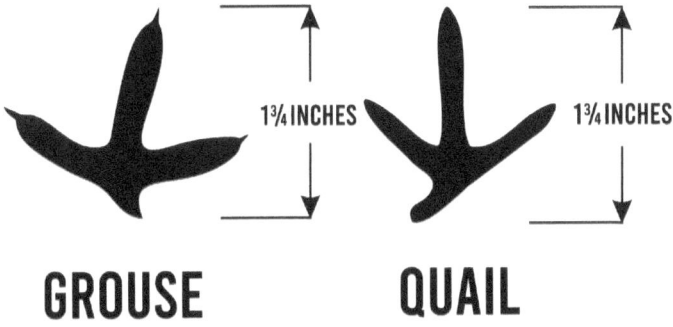

Birds that tend to spend most of their life on the ground have three toes pointing forward in a W-like shape, while they may have one small toe pointing backward, though this may be completely missing in some upland birds. When escaping predators, these birds prefer to fly for short distances and run for most. Their track patterns tend to be alternative—one track followed by another ahead of it—in a straight line as they move. Another sign that you may notice is the dusting bowls. To rid themselves of parasites on their skin or feathers, these birds will burrow with their underbellies into the soft sand to smother or remove them. The size of these dust bowls is dependent on the species creating them. Any lost feathers you find while hunting down the birds will also help you determine what species is in the area. Unless you are using dogs that will help point out or flush these birds from their hiding spot, you will need to do a lot of walking and keeping your eyes open to find them.

DUCKS

Like most birds that do not roost in trees, ducks also have three forward-facing toes. They have no toes facing backward but rather have webbing between each of the toes. You can often find these tracks along muddy banks, but they can be a little challenging to follow, as the ducks do like to wander around quite a bit and create a maze of tracks that are difficult to read. When walking in a straight line, ducks have an alternative pattern to their tracks. Feathers in the area may also give you a clue about where the animals are bedding down for the night.

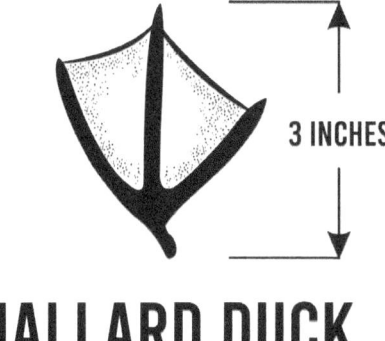

MALLARD DUCK

When hunting ducks, you want the animal to come to you, as shooting it over the water without a dog to retrieve it is nothing more than a wasted kill. It will sink if you do not retrieve it quickly. This is why many hunters prefer to lie in wait for ducks with buffs or among decoys while they sit in camouflage clothing with calls. It is illegal to bait most animals in America, so don't even think of it as a way to attract ducks. Another way to track ducks is to become familiar with their migration patterns and then look into the sky to locate them.

> (Tip: By following the general direction that ducks fly in, you will be able to find their natural feeding areas and can thus stalk them from a vehicle for some distance before continuing on foot.)

TURKEY

The turkey is also an upland bird, but its tracks are significantly bigger than the grouse, partridge, and quail. Its tracks—three toes point forward, with the middle toe being considerably larger than the others—can be as large as four inches. The males have larger feet than the females. As these birds do roost at night, they have a longer fourth toe—which isn't always seen in the tracks—pointing backward to help grip the tree branch while they sleep. When leaping down from the trees, the tracks will show a side-by-side formation of the feet—similarly to birds that hop when moving from one place to another—but when it starts to move away, the tracks start to alternate.

WILD TURKEY

Other signs you can look for are the salad bowl-sized dust bowls they create and the wing drag marks the gobblers (males) create when facing off against a rival, as well as the scratchings as they look for food.

As with all birds that you track, the open ends of the toes point in the direction that the bird is going, so it is important to count the toes to ensure that you are going the right way. Turkey droppings can also identify which of the genders left it behind. This is very important to a hunter as the gender allowed to be hunted for a specific season can then be identified and then tracked. The males tend to leave long droppings—about two inches in length—that form a

J-like shape. This is because they are always on the move and don't even stop to do their business. The hens, however, don't move as much and tend to leave piles that are curled more than the males' droppings.

BULLFROG

No surprise, but bullfrogs are also hoppers, and when they are moving around, their hind feet will land either next to their forefeet or slightly in front of them. The hind feet end in five bulbous toes, and the forelegs end in four, with both feet being webbed for swimming. The forefeet are slightly turned inward while the hind feet are turned outward. Depending on how soft the mud is, you may be lucky enough to see the webbing of the feet, but this is not always the case, and you are more likely only to see the toes. Sometimes you can even see the belly imprint as the creature hops from place to place. (Tip: As they like to be buried in the mud or floating in the water when not looking for food, you may have to disturb their area a little to help locate them if your eyes are not that sharp.)

BULLFROG

SNAPPING TURTLE

Snapping turtles have massive feet and claws, so their tracks are obvious to see, and the size of the print will depend on the animal's age. With five claws in the back and four in the front, it isn't just their beak that can hurt you if you do not handle these creatures with the respect they deserve. As the turtle moves on land, you will mostly see its claws and not the webbing as well as the drag marks from its underbelly and its tail. Scat from this animal is usually found in soft, loose, and pie-like forms on land, and if it is in the water, it simply washes away and is rarely seen. These turtles like to hide during the day when tired and come out at night. When hiding, they burrow into the mud along the edges of their watery home, creating a bowl-like shape that rises from the mud. A hunter with a sturdy stick can push it through the mound, and if it makes contact with a shell, there is a distinct knocking sound.

TURTLE

OTHER POSSIBLE SIGNS

As you are hunting small game, don't miss the opportunity to scout for the larger game for the next season. By noting these tracks, you can make plans to revisit the area once you have the confidence built up to hunt the larger animals.

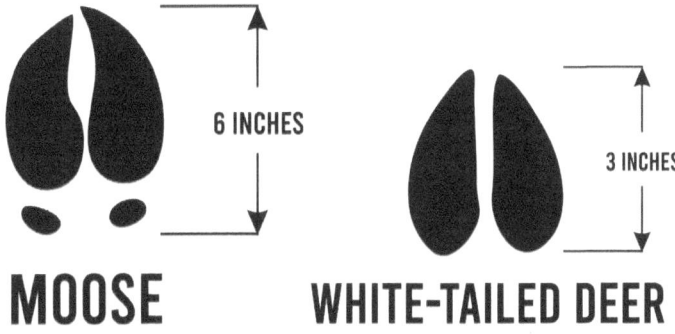

The moose can be particularly dangerous, so try to avoid them unless you are actively hunting them. They can and do kill humans every year, so be cautious. Although the white-tailed deer and moose prints are similar, you cannot overlook the sheer size difference.

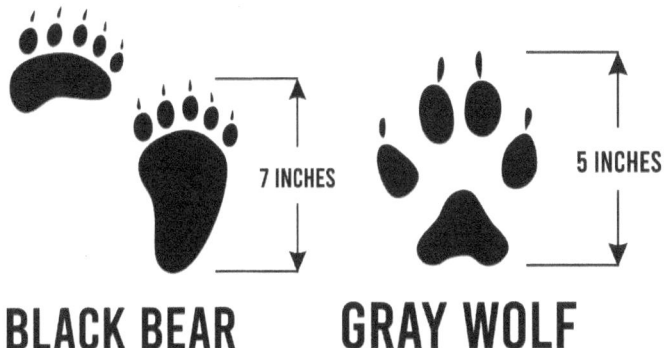

Not just that, but if there are predators in the area that you are not prepared to come across and want to avoid, you can do so by going in the opposite of the tracks. Although most predators will not attack a human directly if there are youngsters in the area, you are exposing yourself to a possible attack. Let this be the warning the animal may not give you.

CHAPTER 6

BETTER SCOUT MORE THAN YOU HUNT

Learning how to scout is the best tool in a hunter's bag of tricks. Being able to understand the nature of animals makes hunting them far easier and more enjoyable. Instead of walking for hours and getting nothing, you can keep your eyes peeled for little hints about what has been moving through the area. Whether you are tracking squirrels or rabbits, you might notice signs of other animals that you may get more enjoyment from hunting and just so happen to have the correct tags.

It also prevents you from becoming single-minded in your endeavor to only concentrate on one thing. You are not the only person out there that is tracking, and you are not the only predator. By keeping a wary eye out, you can keep yourself in the hunter's seat and not become prey yourself to animals like mountain lions, bears, and even wolves. By knowing your prey and their habits, you will know what they do to survive and therefore have an opportunity to see into their lives and build a mental picture of their potential movements and needs. Scouting allows you to stalk and find prey, but it is not easy and requires a lot of practice to hone this particular skill.

SCOUTING FROM A DISTANCE

Scouting does not start when you hit the trail with all your gear. If this is how you plan on scouting, there will be a lot of walking in your future. Whether you are hunting deer or rabbits, you need to know where they are before stumbling into the wilderness. Not just that, but you also need to know and become familiar with the terrain that you will be moving through before you start to do that. Unless you are a veteran hunter that has decades of notes and maps of their best hunting spots, you will need to start your scouting adventure behind the screen of a computer.

Suppose you are going to make use of public hunting grounds. In that case, you will need to identify the best possible place where your prey may be roaming. You can do that through viewing aerial photos, Google Earth, or simply taking the time to join a hunter's forum to get the necessary information from those that have years of experience under their belts. Many hunters will be willing to share a rough estimate of where some of the better hunting grounds are, but don't expect them to tell you where their best hunting spots are, as that is usually a closely guarded secret. You can even make use of resources like YouTube to see the kind of terrain you are likely to find where your particular prey may be hiding. However, keep in mind that those 20-minute videos are usually made after days of scouting, stalking, and finding the perfect opportunity to take the prey. They make a long process look easy, and it doesn't always give the whole scope of the hunt.

Scouting digitally gives a person from out of state/province an opportunity to look at what the general hunting area will look like. You may need to factor in seasonal changes depending on where you are hunting and when you started your digital scouting. Although you could spot terrain perfect for hunting, remember that you are not the only one with this information. Thousands are looking at the same data as you. You will need to plan accordingly if several people want to hunt the same area, so be sure to scout several locations. Having several sites to visit will help you avoid areas that other hunters saturate.

You can also have a partner that can look at the photos and give their own opinion on what they see, and the two of you can work together to choose the best place to hunt. You can even pull in a veteran hunter to help you with some tips and tricks, but be sure to treat them to a hot coffee as thanks for parting with the knowledge. However, no matter how well you scout online or from photos, it is not good to rely solely on this information, as you will have no idea what is happening on the ground. Your next step is to put boots on the ground and scout in person off-season as well as while you hunt.

SCOUTING OFF-SEASON

This is not always possible for a hunter that has to travel to a different state/province, but it is a valued experience that you should not turn your nose up at. Having boots on the ground allows you to see what the terrain is like, which may not have been clear from the aerial photos. Knowing the animal habits you are planning on hunting will give you the edge to your hunting, as you will know what to look for as you walk the vicinity. As you are hiking and looking around, be sure to mark areas of interest on your map so that you can return to them when the season is in full swing.

Check all the potential areas you have identified as points of interest in your online searches to see what the physical location looks like. In reality, these areas may no longer be as good as they appeared online, but now you can scout better areas while you are there. This is how you gain experience. Everything is a learning opportunity. There is no such thing as the perfect hunting ground. Animals keep moving to find better feeding, mating, and resting areas, and you will need to move after them to learn of these places so that you can always find them. Hunting is about more scouting than actually pulling a trigger or laying traps. If you do not know the land and your particular prey's habits, you will never get an opportunity to have one in your sight while you aim.

SCOUTING WHILE HUNTING

If you plan on scouting during your hunting trip, be prepared to lose many hours or even days finding the perfect spot. Try to hunt in the mornings and evenings while scouting around midday, as this is when most animals are not active. Don't assume that you will always get to bag your prey on your first day—though this is a possibility—as you may need to stalk certain prey if you are not sitting and waiting for it to come to you. However, it is not only animal signs you need to note when scouting but also human signs. If there are many cars parked in the vicinity, you know there are other hunters on the trail, and you will need to be careful.

Another critical thing to remember is that tracks belong to no one. Just because you noticed them doesn't mean the animal at the end of them belongs to you. Use some common courtesy, and don't stalk an animal that is already—and obviously—being stalked by another hunter. Suppose you are using ambush tactics for animals, and there are other hunters in the area. In that case, it is a good idea to move at least 100 yards from them so as not to impact their hunting experience. Remember, animals don't like too much activity—especially from humans—so seek to avoid other people by hunting deeper into the wilderness.

This can be a double-edged sword, though. Heading deeper into the wilderness may yield higher success, but if you are hunting larger prey—say turkeys—you may find carrying your prize back a tedious task that takes a lot out of you. This is especially true for people who hunt larger animals such as deer, elk, and bears. As you are wandering around, always be aware of boundaries to the properties in the vicinity. The best way to prevent accidental trespassing is to contact all the private landowners and make them aware of your presence and get the necessary permission to be on their property. If this is not possible, always check and recheck your map to ensure you are where you are supposed to be.

Then, after all that hard work, you have a successful hunt. Congratulations, but keep the celebrations down as much as possible. You may have been lucky, but someone else may still be trying, and you do not want to ruin their opportunity. This is just common courtesy, after all. Another courtesy is that you do not dress (butcher) your kill on the path where others may see it. Move away from where others may be. This brings us to the final point of scouting. Pick up after yourself! No true hunter leaves trash in their wake, only their footprints.

> (Tip: These are general scouting tips that can be used on a variety of animals, but for them to work specifically on the animal you want to hunt, you will also need to incorporate what you know about them to find, stalk, and ambush them.)

SQUIRRELS

Squirrels love white oak acorns but will not turn up their nose at any other nut source. If you want to find squirrels, then find their food source. Once you have noted their food source, look to see if there are signs of squirrels such as tracks or husks of nuts that have already been eaten. If there is a stable food source, they will not go far, and you can simply sit and wait for them to return in case you have spooked them with your entrance into their territory. Nuts are not the only food that they use, so look for patches of edible mushrooms and berries they may eat.

Squirrels spook easily, so hunt them slowly. Take a few steps, then listen. Squirrels make a lot of noise, such as gnawing, dropping nuts, or scampering along branches. Even if you do not hear any close to you, you will be able to listen to some farther away and can therefore stalk them. Even when spooked, squirrels will return to where there is food. You just need to be patient.

Take a seat and wait. If you have a pair of binoculars, now is the time to take them out and scout the area to see where possible squirrels are hiding in trees watching you. If you are quiet and limit your movement, these animals will return to the area within about 40 minutes or so. Line up your shot when you have selected your target, and then take it.

If you want to continue hunting squirrels after taking a shot—either successful or not—you can move to another location a few hundred yards away and try your luck again. Squirrels are active around sunrise and sunset and will actively avoid being out and about during bad weather.

RABBITS

Sadly, with the way humans are encroaching on wild animals' territories, the vast grasslands for hunting rabbits are few and far between. You will have to use a technique called leapfrogging to move from place to place when looking for rabbits or hares. Scouting rabbits is relatively easy using binoculars from a car when driving along roads close to fields and farms. The best time to do this is during dawn and dusk. If you notice rabbits on private property—especially on farms—speak to the farmer about what you have seen. Most farmers will only be too happy to have a rabbit problem disappear without them having to do anything about it. Offering to share the spoils of your hunt wouldn't be a bad gesture on your part as a thank you.

When you have permission to go onto the land, scout it as well. Look for areas that contain brush, fallen treetops, or even brush piles for where rabbits like to hide. Many things eat rabbits, so they are likely to hide and stay hidden until disturbed. You will need to drive them into more open areas to get better opportunities to take them accurately. These animals' coats offer excellent camouflage, so they may be difficult to spot. Don't look for a body; look for the eyes. Glossy spheres are not seen in nature, so if you see them, you know you have a rabbit. If you spot a rabbit this way, you can make use of the spot-and-stalk method, getting just close enough to take an accurate shot.

Rabbits can be tricky to flush on your own. Still, if you use the stop-and-go method, it is a great way to stress the animal into fleeing from you if you have not seen a rabbit take a few heavy steps and then wait. Rabbits can't handle that pressure; if they think they have been spotted, they will bolt. When they do this, you can take a shot. However, some rabbits will try to hold on until your back is to them. Then, they will scamper off to safety, or when they flee successfully, they will try to circle back to avoid you. Always glance over your shoulder now and again to see if any rabbits have done this. Similar to squirrels, if you have flushed all the rabbits and can't spot them anymore, then stop, sit down, and wait for them to return to the safe area.

UPLAND BIRDS

Although the tracks of most upland birds look the same, their natural habitats are all a little different, and this will aid you in scouting them. As these birds are shot on the wing, it is a good idea to practice skeet shooting. This practice will allow you to focus on hitting a moving target that travels through the air. The use of well-trained pointers and receivers is generally permitted when hunting these animals but not required. With a bit of leg work on your part, you can do this alone or with a human partner.

Grouse

These birds like to make use of young forests as homes. These types of forests have different plants that can offer them the cover required to avoid predators. You are more likely to find grouse coverts—where the birds like to congregate—at the edges of different land transitions. This could be an old forest leading into a new one or a path with gravel splits a forest. Grouse like to eat grit from these paths, so make a note if you see one.

To find a grouse, you will need to look for the food they like to eat. As the season changes, so do their food source, so look for different plants, berries, and seeds that are in season. Grouse can camouflage well, and without a dog to point them out, it will take some walking for you to be able to find them. To flush out a grouse from hiding, try the stop-and-go method of hunting. Wait about 30 seconds to a minute before starting to move again. Nervous grouse will leap into the air as they attempt to flee—though some will run—and this will be your opportunity to take a shot. Very rarely will you get a chance to aim and shoot with pinpoint accuracy. If a shot was unsuccessful, move to a new area.

Partridge

Partridge, like the chukar, like to have rocky outcrops to hide in and duck away from most predators. These structures offer crevices where they can find food as well as various places to hide. They will also hide their nests under different bushes, such as sage or greasewood, but any bushy vegetation will do. These birds like to be active in the early morning before moving into shaded areas to wait out the heat of the day. Their roosting spots are generally in steep areas that prevent predators from just sneaking up on them while they sleep.

These birds are easily stalked if you have a set of binoculars that can point out roosting or feeding areas from a distance. They are also quite chatty birds and will communicate with other birds in their convoy, so keep your ears sharp. You can even make use of a call to get birds close to you to respond. Then, it is a simple stop-and-go until the bird flushes out.

As the partridge is prone to flying down a hill and running up, the best way to hunt it is to approach it from higher ground and wait for it to fly up. As you will be shooting downhill, this may affect your aim, so get some practice in this way of shooting. If you have a dog with you, have it chase the birds toward you. Don't be too concerned if your shot misses, as there are other convoys in the vicinity. Move further up and circle around, continuing the stop-and-go method until you find your next target.

Quail

These little birds like different habitats depending on both the weather and what time of the day it is. You are likely to see several quail after it rains as they like to eat the bugs that come out. Due to this, the best time to hunt them is after some rain and the wind has calmed down considerably. If it is in the morning or late afternoon, you will likely find them in open fields looking for food to eat. If this is the case, you can stalk them until you are ready to take the shot. During midday, the birds prefer to hide in wooded areas—where there are briar patches—as predators or hunters can't spot them. At night, they are asleep in the long grass.

When looking over fields that may hold quail, look at the length and thickness of the grass. If it is too short or too thick, they do not like to enter it, as they will either be spotted or cannot move through it. As with the other upland birds, the stop-and-go method is the best to spook the bird into flight so that you can take a snapshot at it. Always make use of some binoculars if you want to scout a field without entering it, as you do not want the birds to flee into wooded areas where it is difficult to flush them out on your own.

DUCKS

There are several ways to stalk ducks, depending on your particular style of hunting. If you prefer your prey to come to you, then make use of a blind that you can hide in a while using duck calls and decoys in the body of water you are hunting on. Ducks are more likely to use bodies of water that already contain ducks, as they are pretty social. If you want to be out on the water yourself, you can row a boat into the middle of a large body of water and then sit with the decoys and use the calls. This is called float hunting. However, when shooting a duck over the water, there is a chance that the body becomes difficult to retrieve, especially if you do not have a retriever dog. Unfortunately, the blind setup and decoys can make for a costly hunt, so because of this, most hunters prefer the stop-and-stalk method—also known as jump shoot—which is significantly cheaper.

When you are moving more, you can identify multiple possible places where ducks like to feed, wander, or roost during the night. Ducks will use any body of water which includes places like ditches next to the road or dugout areas on farms, so always keep an eye out when traveling for potential areas that may contain duck-friendly water locations. When you spot a possible feeding area for ducks, use a pair of binoculars to see if any ducks hang around. When you spot them, you can steadily make your way toward them but will need to start stalking within 100 yards of the birds. If you have cover closer to your prey, all the better, but if not, take it slow and drop to your belly. Once you are within a range, you are comfortable taking a shot. Then, you can stand up to reveal yourself. This should cause the ducks to flush, but if they don't, then just make some kind of noise to alert them. As they flush, aim for a duck along the edges of the group, and aim for the body to avoid shooting over or under the animal. If you missed your shot, the animals would likely return after a while, as they will need to continue to feed. This is usually easier if there is some cover for you to meld back.

When the animals are feeding, they are not always alert, so it is easier to sneak up on them. When they are wandering, closer toward the afternoon, they will be more on high alert, as they will be socializing with other ducks. If you miss a shot at this time, they are likely not to return. Shooting at ducks that are getting ready to roost poses the problem of accidentally shooting outside of the state or province's regulations. Many hunters like to set alarms for themselves that will stop them from exceeding this time limit.

Retrieval of your successful hunt can be tricky with a duck, as you would prefer to shoot the animal over the land, but this is not always the case. You cannot leave a potentially wounded animal to drown or wander deeper into the brush, so make sure to follow up as soon as you can.

TURKEY

Hunting turkey can be done in two ways. Hide in a blind with decoys and turkey callers or walking out on foot in turkey country. Both of these have their pros and cons. Turkeys have excellent eyesight, and with one false step, they will be gone in a blink of an eye. The first step to a successful turkey hunt is that you wear the appropriate camouflage for the season. The next is to decide which type of call you will use. The two most popular hands-free varieties are the mouth (diaphragm) call and the friction call. The mouth call can be purchased and held inside the mouth and will remain silent until you create the correct shape of your tongue to make the sounds required. This is something that will need to be practiced to produce the proper sounds necessary. The friction call can be made with a magnet—a product called the magnetic push/pull box call—that can be placed on the side of the shotgun and then moved when a call is required. These calls are needed, as you will need to get the turkey to come to you. Do not make calls too often, as this can cause turkeys to become wary of you.

When using a blind, make sure to set it up in an area not under a roosting tree. Turkeys move away from their roosting spots, so they may not want to hang around after waking up. Make sure you have the appropriate, natural cover around you. You want to see the turkey coming toward you, but you don't want the turkey to know where you are. Set your decoy turkeys within the range of your gun and slightly off-center of where you are. You want the wild turkey to focus on them and not your possible movement.

If you are stalking in an open country, do so slowly, and don't let a turkey spot you before you spot it. Make use of cover when you notice it, and use your calls to bring it closer. Suppose you have managed to spook the turkey you are hunting. In that case, you may have to give the area about 30 minutes of silence and no movement before starting again. If no turkey answers your call, you will have to go through to a new location and begin again. Stick to infrequent calls until you hear an answer.

Depending on the season you are hunting in, you may have to use different calls to attract the different genders. When making the gobble sound, you are likely to attract large males who see you as competition and chase the smaller males away. The yelp sound imitates a female and will attract the males to you without chasing any away. The cluck sound is the most well-known sound—plus the easiest to perform—and will attract both genders.

BULLFROG

Bullfrogs can be hunted by day or by night, depending on your state or province's regulations. Different people have different ways to hunt bullfrogs, so you will have to pick your preferred method. Stalking a bullfrog by day is relatively easy, as they can be spotted resting on the banks of their watery home or have the top of their heads—with their huge eyes—just above the water looking at you. If you cannot see the bullfrogs, then listen for their croaks. You can scan the water with a flashlight or headlamp at night, and you will notice the eyes. By the eyes' size, you can judge the size of the frog and distinguish it from other animals such as alligators.

If you plan to hunt with a gun, aim for the head and watch where the body lands, as the frogs will be knocked back by the blast. This can cause you to lose your meal if you lose sight of it in the water. Most states/provinces don't allow for hunting with guns at night, so be sure to check the regulations before going frogging.

Many hunters also like to catch frogs by hand, but this can cause a considerable disturbance in the water and can cause several other frogs to flee from you. This, however, could still be a fun way to hunt and teach younger hunters how to catch a meal with no equipment. Then, there is the art of gigging. A gig is a pronged spear which is a well-known method of hunting frogs. This spear can be thrust into the body of the frog either from a boat or as you stalk them through the water. Be sure to aim for the head where possible for an ethical shot. If you like the idea of fishing, you can also try to hook a frog. Tying a red piece of fabric around the hook and dangling it around the frog will cause it to try to eat it as the fabric mimics the appearance of an insect.

If you are hunting these animals at night, be sure not to cross in front of the light you are shining on them, as this will spook them. Once scared, they will hop into the water and be gone within seconds. You may find that you will need waders to truly enjoy hunting bullfrogs.

SNAPPING TURTLE

Avoid the head and go for the tail! This cannot be stressed enough, as their beak will take a finger if you are not careful. Once you have located a snapping turtle pond or habitat, there are many ways to get them out. If you are fearless, you can dive into the water with snorkeling gear and pick them out of the mud to place them in a boat. Also, you can set up traps that have a one-way opening. These traps are usually made of chicken wire and measure at about two feet in width and height with four feet in length. The bait—usually a meat source—should be placed at the back of the trap to entice the turtle through the trap entrance that won't allow it out. The trap needs to be anchored to the shore very firmly—with part of it sticking out of the water—as a trapped turtle is likely to struggle. If your state/province allows trapping, ensure that you are checking this daily to prevent a loss of your prey.

You can also try to hook these ancient beasts if you have the strength to do so. You will need a turtle hook—baited with some meat—and some thick cord that needs to be tied securely to the hook, as well as a big jug or similar floating device. This floating device also needs to be tied to something that will prevent it from floating away once the turtle has taken the bait. You can leave this device up overnight if you wish. You do not want to use a fishing line, as trying to pull the turtle up will cause the line to bite into your hands. Ideally, the turtle will go for the bait, take the hook, and then swim back down because of the floating device. Turtles will usually head toward land if they cannot swim back down into the mud. You should then easily be able to find the turtle when you return in the morning. Once you have the turtle, you will need to catch it physically. The beak needs to be occupied while you aim to grab the tail. Some people will end the kill immediately by shooting the turtle—or otherwise removing the head—while others prefer to keep the turtle alive for a few days to clean it in some fresh water and continue to feed it fresh meat or plant matter until you are ready to harvest it.

These animals prefer to feed at night and can be noted in the water by their heads and eyes that stick out of it. Look along the mud banks and fallen trees close to water to see signs that these animals are in the vicinity you are hunting.

CHAPTER 7

PRACTICE MAKES A MASTER

Simply having all this knowledge at your fingertips—or even in your brain—is not enough. You need to put into practice what you have been taught so far. You can't hope to get a perfect heart shot if you have never pulled a trigger in the past. Do you know how to clear a jammed weapon? How to set a snare? Not yet. Practicing the skills taught to you so far will mean the difference between a perfect, well-executed shot and a lost opportunity. Ensure that you are practicing correctly so that you are as close to perfect as possible. Each hunter does develop their way of doing things, but that doesn't mean that you are doing something wrong. Start with the basics, practice, and keep practicing those skills until they are second nature to you.

HOW TO BE A BETTER HUNTER

Hunting is a physical sport, and you will need to be fit to go for larger and larger game. Carrying a few squirrels home doesn't seem like much, but when you eventually bag a deer, you will have to take that back to your car, and deer are heavy! An excellent point to start before hunting is to get your body ready for extended walking with a weight. Taking an extended hike with your fully packed backpack is a way to build up your endurance and fitness. Start small and slowly build up the distance.

Learn to pack your gear correctly so that you are never overloaded in a hunt. Create a checklist to ensure that you have all the vital tools necessary for a hunt. Once you have this ready to go, pack the bag and see how it feels. Too heavy? See how you can rearrange items and what you can carry on yourself instead of in your bag. Perhaps some items can be combined to lessen the space taken up, such as wrapping duct tape around other items instead of just chucking a roll into your bag.

Take a few first aid courses and get certified to know how to handle any situation you may find yourself in. Practice on people—who are hopefully not injured—to gain confidence in your skills. Even if you don't get certified, be sure to know how to use all the items in your first aid kit, and learn how to build one yourself instead of relying on a standard kit you just buy.

When you are on these hikes, take the time to look for tracks and signs of animals in the vicinity. This gives you ample opportunity to study tracks and learn to identify the animals in your region. If you are not yet familiar with the tracks, take a book about tracks with you so that you can learn as you go. A great place to look for clear tracks is in the mud close to riverbanks.

Consider camping overnight so that you can test your wilderness skills, such as making a fire from scratch or creating a shelter from the resources around you. Do check the rules and regulations of the park you wish to camp in, and follow all their safety guides to ensure that you remain safe while doing this. If you are planning on fishing or trying your hand at hunting small game on this trip, ensure that you have the necessary licenses to do this without getting possible fines. Take the time to scout while you are hiking. The more information you gather about the location you are in, the better.

The quality of your equipment is something you need to consider. Although you do not need the top-of-the-line merchandise for hunting, you need to be able to weed out poor-quality goods by testing them rigorously. Learn how to repair equipment that could break, and keep your gear in good working order. Even if you are not hunting, always be prepared. Quality gear is pricey, so start with the slightly cheaper gear and save toward the more expensive if this will become a hobby you intend to keep doing every year. If something new comes out—and it is affordable—test it out to see if it measures up to what you expect of it. Never buy something that looks cool but has no actual function, as it will only weigh you down.

Don't stick to only one type of weapon. Branching out and using multiple hunting tools allows you to sharpen various skills that can impact which tools you use. Using a slingshot will enable you to hone your stalking skills which will, in turn, make it easier to sneak up on the larger game when you use your rifle. Knowing how to use different weapons can also extend your hunting season, as you can easily switch from hunting with a rifle, a shotgun, or even a muzzleloader. Clean your tools! This isn't just your guns but also your knives. Keep barrels clean and clear and knives free of blood. Dirty equipment lowers their durability and their functionality.

Use any and every possible resource you can to get better, whether that is going to the range to practice with a weapon or scouring the forums for people to help you with questions. Read books, speak to people, and even go on hunts with other veteran hunters to gain vital experience without having to pull the trigger. If you do pull that trigger and miss, don't think of it as a failure. Think of it as a learning opportunity. When you miss a shot, think about what went wrong and how you can correct it for the next time you can line up a shot. Not all hunts end with an animal in the bag. Learn to accept this.

If you do succeed in a hunt, learn how to do it ethically. An ethical shot is a clean shot that puts an animal down quickly and with little to no pain. Better for it and better for the meat left behind. Practice how to skin and gut (dress) an animal after it has been shot so that you harvest what is needed without losing any of the good parts. With larger animals, there are many ways to dress them—such as gutless versus retaining gut while dressing—so practice which suits you better. Take a friend. The easiest way to learn is through teaching, and we know that two heads are better than one.

Lastly, treat the land and animals with respect. Do not take potshots at animals. Aim for a clean shot that prevents injury. Pick up your trash and dispose of it properly. This includes guts, packaging, and other possible waste. If you meet other hunters, you can swap stories, but you shouldn't hunt their area. Common courtesy will see you making friends with people who are willing to share their tips and tricks of the trade.

SHARPENING SPECIFIC SKILLS

Some skills need to be perfected over time and are something that needs to be practiced. Something like turkey and duck calls need to be perfected to get the animals to come to you, and you need to get good at this to improve your hunting chances. Other skills, such as learning how to set a snare, won't just enhance your arsenal of taking an animal—it may someday save your life when you have no other choice.

Bird Calls

When making use of bird calls, it isn't just about making a sound but how you make the sound. Each call is different and means different things to the birds. By practicing with the call, you can imitate a welcoming call, a mating call, or a feeding call, all of which the wild animals will listen for and decide whether they want to be enticed or not. Speak to veteran hunters of these animals to learn how they use the respective calls to attract potential prey and learn from them.

Don't know anyone who is an expert? Simply look online where videos are posted that teach you how to make the calls with various types of equipment. Once you have the basics down, you can practice out in nature. However, be wary of where you practice, as turkeys have a great capacity to learn. You can inadvertently teach them how to avoid hunters in the future.

When practicing your turkey calls, go to an area where no hunting is allowed. You can communicate with these animals using the yelps, purrs, and a variety of other sounds. If you are consistently getting replies—whether from humans or other turkeys—you are doing something right. This is something that takes a while to perfect, so keep at it with the various tools that are available for this.

Making Snares

Unless you are in a situation where you need to survive, ensure that snare usage is legal before using them. Practicing making them is not illegal, so take the time to get familiar with the basic setup of the common snare. To make the snare, you will need a picture hanging wire or snare wire and something to cut the wire—some people like to use a 24-gauge steel wire, but the preference is up to you.

Cut about an 18 inch to a two-foot piece of wire loose from the spool. At the one end of the wire, create a loop—about the size of your thumb pad—and then twist it around the wire, allowing it to get smaller and smaller until you have twisted enough so that it won't unravel.

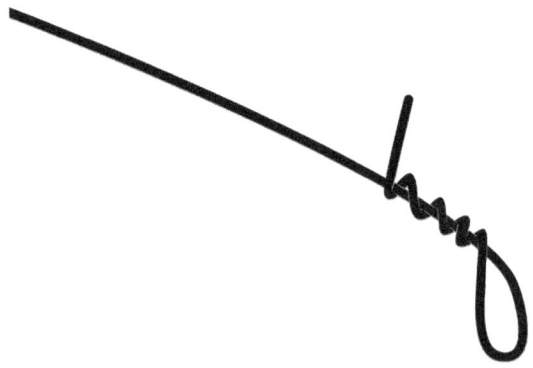

This is called a slip loop, and you now have to feed the other end of the wire through it to make the noose. You can then decide to leave the other end open or to create a larger slip loop to be used as an anchor point that you can drive a stake through. If you leave it untied, then you can tie it to an anchor when you are ready to do so.

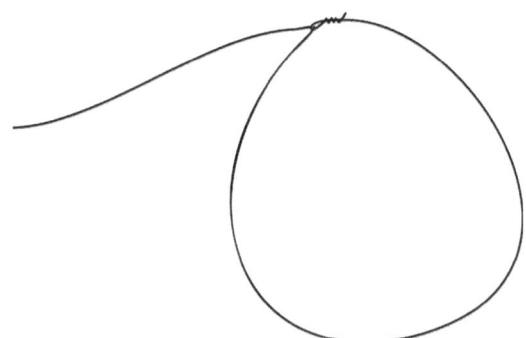

The size of the noose will depend on the animal that you are hunting. If you are hunting rabbits or hares, then the noose size should be the size of your fist. Any smaller and the rabbit will just move it aside, and any larger can cause it to hop through or have its back legs caught instead of its neck. This can lead the animal to suffer when caught, which needs to be avoided. If you are hunting squirrels, you will need to make it smaller, or the prey will simply just hop through it.

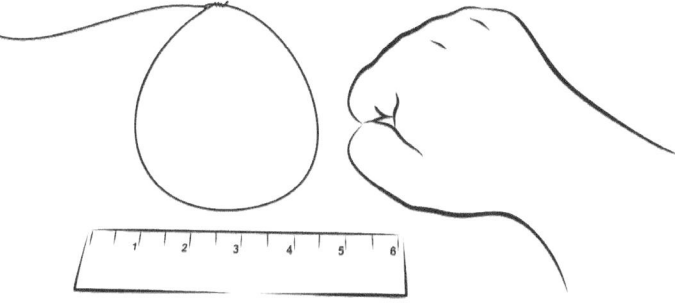

Making a snare is the easy part. Anyone can do it, and the skill comes in knowing where to place the snare to be most effective.

Setting Snares

For a snare to be accurate, you need to know how your prey thinks and where it likes to move. By knowing that, you will be able to set the snare so that the prey will head toward it without knowing it is there, as you are using the natural runs that the animals use. Scout the area to see where these animals are moving from cover to cover, and set the snare in its path where a natural tunnel is formed. The snares will need to be anchored to something that cannot be uprooted, as you want the animal to be caught and not run away with the trap attached to it.

Once the snare is set—a little off the ground—then look to prevent the animal from simply going around it. Prey are very clever, more than we give them credit for. Any open spaces around the snare need to be eliminated. You can do this by putting sticks in the ground or snow so that gaps are closed, and the only way for the animal to get through to their hiding area is to go through the space where the snare is set. If you want to prevent the animal from jumping over the snare, you may need to put a branch in the way. Leave the snare for several hours while you set up a few more.

If a snare hasn't caught something in a few days, you will need to read the tracks to see why this is so. There could be a gap that the animal has gone through your funnel, or they have jumped over or simply moved the snare out of the way. You must adjust to the animal's intelligence. Sometimes you may find a still-living animal in the snare, and you will need to dispatch it as ethically and quickly as possible. Do not try to remove the snare from a living animal, as they will do everything in their power to escape, including biting and kicking.

Another type of snare you can make use of is the spring snare. To set this snare, you will need a sapling that you can bend over that is close to the animal's run, two pieces of wood (one longer than the other) that can be connected to each other through a notch close to the ends, your prepared wire snare, and another piece of wire that will be connecting the tree to your trap. You can drive the longer of the two pieces of wood into the ground next to the run. This is your anchor point for the trap. Tie the spare wire to the bent-over sapling and connect the smaller notched pieces of wood. Attach the snare to this piece of wood as well before setting the trap by placing the two notched pieces of wood together. The wire connected to the tree needs to be taut but not so taut that it rips the anchor point out. Once the trap is correctly set up, make sure that the snare stays open over the run. You can achieve this by adding a few smaller and weaker sticks to keep it open. You can also create a funneling effect that was used with the regular snare, but it must not interfere with the trap's ability to be sprung when the animal gets snared. Instead of the animal remaining trapped on the ground to be picked off by predators, this trap, once sprung, hoists the animal into the air to keep it out of reach of most predators. With this kind of trap, you can notice if it has been triggered or not from a distance and can therefore prevent you from checking the area too frequently and scaring off potential prey.

> (Tip: Once a snare has done its purpose, please remove it from the area to not catch unfortunate animals that you will not use.)

Making and Setting a Deadfall Trap

There are several deadfall traps that you can make use of. Some are simpler in design, while others are more complex. For this book, we will be looking at the Paiute deadfall trap. To make this trap, you need several components, which are the large flat rock, a short vertical post stick, string or cord, the longer angle stick, the trigger component, stick for the trigger (sticks need to be as straight as possible), and some bait the rodent of choice may like (berries, nuts, or seeds). The angle and vertical sticks should be the thickness of your thumb, but this will depend on the weight of the rock you are using. If the rock causes these sticks to bow under the weight, then you will need stronger sticks. The trigger stick needs to be thinner than the vertical and angle sticks but strong enough to hold the trap without setting it off. The string can be made of cotton or a fishing line, but alternatively, you can also braid plant matter together to create a cord if you have none.

Find a sturdy, straight stick to create your vertical post and angle stick. Cut the vertical stick to have a pointed end (V-shape) at the top and a flat lower end. Now, cut a longer section of the main stick which also ends in a V-shape. Close to this end, cut a notch so that the vertical post stick can fit in it. The angled stick will be supporting the rock and not the vertical post. Next, make the trigger component. This is a thin piece of flat wood (about two inches by one inch) with a hole drilled through one end. The cord goes through this hole and can be knotted in place, or a loop can be created, which can be held in place by a smaller stick through the loop end. The other end of the cord is then tied to the end of the angled stick. You can notch the bottom of this stick to help with keeping the cord attached. Where the cord will wrap around the bottom of the vertical stick, make a notch so that the cord doesn't slip along the stick's length.

Now that all your components are prepped and ready, you can start setting the trap. It may take some practice trying to balance everything and getting the correct lengths to correspond to the weight of the rock, so practice it while you are not in a survival situation. Balance the angled stick on the vertical stick using the notch. Place the rock's edge on the angled stick, making sure the middle edge is over both sticks for balance. Wrap the trigger mechanism around the notch in the vertical post and set the trap by placing the trigger stick against the trigger and the rock and an angle that the trap isn't sprung. When built correctly, the trap should stand by itself, with the angled stick and trigger stick balancing the rock precariously. Once balanced, add some bait on one side of the trigger stick and then leave the trap to do its job.

Rodents are very clever and will sometimes take the bait without setting off the trap. If this happens frequently, you may have to use a thinner trigger stick or change its angle for it to be more sensitive. The Paiute deadfall trap can be made larger if you want to catch animals such as squirrels and rabbits. However, snares are likely best for them to conserve the meat better than a deadfall trap. Deadfall traps are perfect for small game animals that can be used to bait larger traps or hooks for fishing.

Shooting Practice

Whichever weapon you are making use of, you will need to practice with it—not a few days before the hunt but constantly. Keeping your skills sharp is the difference between a meal or going hungry when you should be trying to survive. Even if you aren't in survival mode, keeping your skills honed is something every hunter should do regardless of year.

Some people like to put hours into a range of some sort, and this does have its merits, but it isn't ideal. A range offers a straight shot with only distance as your challenge, and it is not enough when your prey is a moving target. You will need to practice your hunting skills under various conditions such as rain, snow, and wind to get accustomed to what could happen in reality when you are on a hunt. Take care when practicing in your backyard for archery or using a slingshot to ensure that you do not harm anyone around you. Set up targets like tin cans on a string to simulate a moving target. Suppose you have a larger, more rural property. In that case, you can set up 3D animal targets in the brush, on hills, down a hill, any place conceivable to allow you the opportunity to practice difficult shots and stalking.

Practice the way you take your shots. If you mostly shoot standing, then practice shooting from a seated position and vice versa until you can do both. You can even consider shooting on the move to see if this is a skill you can sharpen, though always be sure that your shots are ethical at all times, even against targets. Suppose you practice just to hit the edge of a target. In that case, when it comes to shooting a living animal, it can mean the possibility of a complete miss or an injured animal fleeing in panic and pain to succumb to its wounds much later where you cannot get to it.

Work on your weaknesses until they are your strengths, and learn to leave a shot unfired. One of the most important aspects of hunting is knowing that your shot will find its mark. If you are not sure, you will need to move into a different position to get a better shot or allow the animal to move away. Always aim for a quick and clean kill.

CHAPTER 8

DOMINATE YOUR FIRST HUNT

Before you go out and buy what you think you need to have a successful hunt, consider the order of things you need to do. The first isn't going out to get a gun; though this is an exciting purchase, it really shouldn't be your first. There are many steps to take before setting out for a hunt, so be sure to follow them closely to allow you to get the most from your experience.

PREPARING BEFORE THE HUNT

Before you can even begin to think about hunting, you need to complete your Hunter Ed regardless of whether your state or province requires it or not. By completing this, you will be certified to hunt safely with whatever weapon you choose in whatever state/province you want. If you are new to hunting, you may never have handled a hunting tool before, so it is a good idea to use mentorship programs that can be found in your state/province. The programs allow you to learn from veteran hunters and people who are masters in a specific aspect of hunting. These people can teach you to hunt with different kinds of guns, bows, and other weapons. Not only that, but they are the ones that will invite you on hunts so that you can see one in action without having the pressure of bringing a prize home. By working with a mentor, you learn the necessities of hunting with others, sharing, and respecting the land you are making use of.

Mentors can also share information about their favorite equipment they use to bring their prizes home. They can show you how to do proper field dressing and cleaning of the animal so that you take the best parts of your hard work home. These tips and tricks of the trade cannot be learned in a book but only at the feet of masters, so listen to what they have to say because you have a lot to learn. By being in a mentorship program, you can even pick up a hunting buddy that will make the larger hunts a lot easier to deal with in the future. Once you become a master, think of giving back to the community by teaching young ones the skills you learned and were introduced to. This is how you can keep the tradition of hunting alive.

Many people like to hunt alone, but that doesn't mean that they aren't willing to share information they have gathered over the years. Take the time to join conservation groups and participate in their activities, such as volunteering for cleanup days. Though this doesn't seem appealing to most people, it is a great way for you to come together and speak with like-minded people. From people in these groups, you will be able to gain local information about farmers who are willing to let hunters onto their land, the best spots for hunting certain animals, and even get exposed to people who are eager to teach you more about scouting or tracking.

The biggest asset to a hunter isn't their gear or weapon—it is information. Gather as much knowledge as possible from various sources so that you can form a clear image of what you want from a hunt. Know which hunting seasons lead into another season so that you can combine hunting for one animal while scouting for another. Teach yourself about edible items out in the wild that can be found in the state/province you want to hunt in. With this knowledge, you will live off the land even if you do not harvest from a hunt.

Learn about your state or province's regulations about hunting, get licensed, and then get started on preparing to hunt small game animals. Now is the time to look at the gear and clothing you may need for a hunt. With the knowledge from this book and anything extra from mentors, you will know exactly what is needed in your pack when hunting for certain animals. Purchase what you need, and test it at home before taking it out into the wilderness. Make sure the clothing you get is suited to the weather and regulations of the state/province you are hunting in. Practice with different weapons to see which feels best to use for the animal you want to hunt. Put the hours into learning how to use, clean, and maintain the weapon. Consider learning to use both a firearm and another weapon that isn't a firearm so that you can have access to different game and seasons that you can hunt in. Keep those shooting skills sharp by practicing a few days out of the week during the off-season.

Scout the areas where you will be hunting both digitally and physically, having your boots on the ground. Take the time to look for the tracks in the area, and note possible feeding areas where the animal of choice is likely to show up. Look for places where you could approach from with and without cover. While scouting, you can even make use of practicing your stalking of animals in the region. See how close you can get without alerting the animals.

PREPARING YOURSELF FOR A HUNT

If you want a good hunt, you need to be in great shape to go after prey in a variety of conditions. You will need to get fit and break in your hunting boots and gear. Very few people have the fitness for hiking miles with a fully packed backpack, so start small. Go for a short walk along the flat ground with your new hiking boots so that you can slowly break them in. Then, once they are more comfortable, start stacking those miles on them. Once you can comfortably walk for several miles on flat ground, take up hiking to help you build the endurance for more challenging terrain that will await you on a hunt. Set goals for the distance you want to reach, and when you get those goals successfully time and time again, it is time to start doing the hikes with your hunting gear. Try doing these hikes under various conditions to get the feel of what it will be like when you are on an actual hunt.

However, hunting isn't just about the physical strength of a person but also their mentality. Hunting small game is easier to carry home, but when you are bagging a larger game that requires multiple trips in and out of where you shot it, the brain needs to take over for those tired legs. You need to be mentally strong to handle the weight and the distance to ensure that you bring the whole harvest back home. Hunting takes you out of your comfort zone, so be prepared for sore feet, feeling wet and cold, and possibly being hungry. There is no such thing as an easy hunt. Even if you have one easy hunt, you are likely never to have something like that again.

Hunting can be an emotional roller coaster for some people as well. People who pride themselves as animal lovers struggle with the concept of hunting sometimes, and it does make it difficult for them to enjoy this practice. To overcome this aspect, you will have to go into the hunt with a clear goal of what you want to achieve. This will help you to visualize what you want from a hunt. Remember, you do not have to take the shot if you don't want to or need to. Finding your quarry is just as big a rush as taking it. Please make your choice, and then follow through with it.

PREPARING THE HUNT

By hunting small game, you are guaranteed the possibility of a hunt, as more people are likely competing for the larger game instead of rabbits. Enjoy the fact that you will hunt mostly undisturbed by other hunters. Even the gear required to hunt the smaller animals is cheaper than those required for the larger game. Start by choosing an animal you want to hunt, then check for the various licenses, permits, and other necessities you may need. You won't need a duck call if you are hunting rabbits.

Ensure that the sights—if you are using them—are set and ready to be used. Then, go through your gear and attire to make sure everything is ready to be packed. Only take what is needed so that you do not become encumbered. Come up with a plan on how you see the hunt will go. This will allow you to remain focused on the hunt when it happens and not second-guess yourself about certain decisions. Stick to this plan unless an emergency occurs. Know the limits of your license and the limit of the range you are allowed to hunt on. Suppose you notice that there is a chance of stepping onto private property—phone the owner to get permission.

Hunting starts as soon as you wake on the day of the hunt. Take note of the weather, and consider which animals will be out and about. Once you decide to continue with the day, you need to keep your eyes and ears open to find the prey you want. When an animal is spotted, consider which is the best way to get closer. Play on the animal's nature to help you decide on this. Nervous animals will flush out with a stop-and-go method while animals eating calmly in the distance can be stalked. Patience is more than just a virtue, and it is the lifeblood of a hunter. If you do not have the patience to sit quietly or to stalk prey, then it is best you learn or find another hobby to keep yourself occupied.

When you eventually have that animal lined up in your sight, take the time to ask yourself a few questions. Can I get closer to get a better shot without disturbing the animal? Will this be an ethical shot? Is it safe to fire my weapon? Once you are sure the shot will be ethical, then take it and bag your prize. This is about the quality of your shot, not the quantity. You would rather have three prized rabbits taken with three good shots than three rabbits on you and the fourth suffering in its warren until it expires with a poor fourth shot.

Remain safe at all times. This means being aware of potential dangers in the wilderness, such as other hunters and predators, as well as letting people know about where you are. By ensuring that there are people who know where you are, how long you will be gone, and when you will return, you guarantee that if you cannot get back (for whatever reason), there will be help arriving quickly.

GOING BIGGER

When hunting small game, you can sharpen your skills and build up confidence with each animal you take successfully. However, once your confidence is up, don't fear failure. It is just another learning opportunity that all adds up to a larger hunt. While you are practicing on the small game, see if you can get some tags for larger animals. Getting tags and licenses for areas that are not your own can take some time to do well ahead of the season you want to hunt so doing it this way, you will have the time to prepare when you get those tags. Don't be disappointed if you don't get the tags for the animal you want to hunt, as there are general hunting licenses that still allow you to hunt other animals.

Hunting larger animals comes with more difficulties. They are wary of humans, and you will need to mask your scent to prevent them from noticing you. You will also need to be significantly fitter and stronger to take on these hunts. You will have to walk vast distances and carry any harvested items back with you. Squirrels do not weigh much, but a hind quarter of an elk will be a chore.

It would be best to be wary of the potential diseases that a state/province has that will prevent you from taking certain parts of an animal back with you. There are several states/provinces where animals have become infected with the chronic wasting disease (CWD), which is highly contagious. Get more information about this disease to ensure that you are allowed to keep what you harvest instead of having to waste it. Make contact with the state or province's Fish and Wildlife Service Department to get more information about what to do if you come across an animal with this disease. It is also a good idea to keep an eye out for diseases that can affect you! If there is Lyme disease in the area, ensure you have taken all the precautions necessary to prevent infection from tick bites.

CONCLUSION

This book aims to instill the knowledge of hunting the smaller game available to anyone who wishes to explore the beauty of the American wilderness. Although it isn't an easy task, and you will need to spend some time training your body, this is a sport that anyone can do: man, woman, or child. Hunting is more than just that photograph of you holding your very first prize. It is about accumulating knowledge, being prepared, and knowing how to apply everything you have learned.

The starting point for all new hunters is to take the time to get the Hunter Ed before gathering everything you will need to go out into the wilderness to gain invaluable experience. Whether you are scouting from the air or taking the time to break in some boots with the family on a hike, keep an eye out for hunting locations that will yield the prizes you want from nature. Know your limitations regarding weapons and terrain that you can manage on your first hunt to ensure you get the most from every hunt.

Become familiar with the laws and regulations in your state/province for weapons—as well as snares and traps—as this will ensure that you will not be fined under the guise of "Oh, I didn't know!" As a responsible hunter, you have to ensure that you know the rules. Make an effort to get to know what kind of equipment you will need to have on the hunt, then ask on hunter forums for the opinions of others on the merchandise. Scour the Internet for videos of other people's hunts to learn some tips that you can try to apply to your hunt. A great place to meet like-minded people that enjoy hunting is a Facebook group called, "Hunting for Greatness Community," a community that shares a ton of valuable information about hunting for beginners and veterans alike. Once a member, you will find friendly people who are always willing to help you out with any of your hunting queries.

Ensure that any equipment you intend to use is thoroughly tested before taking it out into the wild, as this is a surefire way to get into trouble if you don't. Practice with any weapons that you will be using, as that is the only way you will improve your skill and establish the quickest and cleanest way to dispatch your prey. Learn the difference between a potential sloppy shot versus a clean kill. Patience is needed on a hunt, but that isn't the only skill you will need. Depending on the weapon of choice, you may have to make use of various stalking and hunting techniques while all the time asking yourself if you are in the correct position to claim a prize or if it is best to watch it move along.

As much as we all hope for a perfect hunt, sometimes disaster can strike, but it doesn't have to remain a disaster if you are fully prepared. By having a personally packed first aid kit, you ensure your safety and your possible survival. By preparing for the worst, you will always be ready for everything. Knowing how to build a shelter, get water, start a fire, and obtain different food sources, you will keep yourself living long enough until professional help can make its way to you.

To efficiently hunt your quarry, you need to understand what it needs from its environment in terms of food and shelter. Once you understand this, you will effortlessly find tracks and signs of where they have been. Keep within your tags and licenses within the scope, as this is what sets a true hunter apart from poachers. To avoid being labeled as a poacher at all times, know where you are so that you are not hunting on property that doesn't allow hunting or is privately owned.

No one is just born a great hunter, so take the time to practice everything you have learned in this book, as it will come in handy one day. Know the tracks. Know the habits. Know the boundaries. Become a better hunter by learning from others and teaching those that ask you questions as you improve at bringing back prized harvests again and again. By starting small, you will gain the confidence to eventually build your hunts up to go after the giants of America: moose, bear, and wolves.

Now that you have read this book from cover to cover, you are ready to go forth and prepare yourself for the great outdoors. No longer will you have to stare longingly at the mountains and feel the jealousy of someone who has a freezer full of fresh meat from a hunt. That can be you. That can be anyone willing to try hunting. Get yourself educated, certified, then gather all the equipment you need, and set forth on your hunting adventure. Nothing is holding you back. Remember, we hunt to live and live to hunt!

REFERENCES

American Expedition. (n.d.). *Quail information, photos, artwork and facts*. Retrieved May 12, 2021, from https://forum.americanexpedition.us/quail-information-facts-photos-and-artwork

Aquachigger. (2015, July 19). *How to find and catch snapping turtles by hand* [Video]. YouTube. https://www.youtube.com/watch?v=fW8CZNH53nE

Archery Country. (n.d.). *What animals are considered small game?* Retrieved May 9, 2021, from https://archerycountry.com/blog/what-animals-are-considered-small-game/

ASG Staff. (2017, September 6). *Honorable kill: Slingshot hunting etiquette*. American Survival Guide. https://www.asgmag.com/survival-skills/survival-hunting-fishing/honorable-kill-slingshot-hunting-etiquette/

Backcountry Chronicles. (n.d.). *Realistic target practice to prepare for the hunt*. Www.backcountrychronicles.com. Retrieved May 17, 2021, from https://www.backcountrychronicles.com/practice-for-the-hunt/

Beasley, K. (2016, October 7). *A beginner's guide to hunting*. Northern Ontario Travel. https://www.northernontario.travel/northeastern-ontario/beginners-guide-to-hunting

Bedrock & Paradox. (2020, January 22). *Great small game hunts of North America (2019 hunting in review)*. https://bedrockandparadox.com/2020/01/22/great-small-game-hunts-of-north-america-2019-hunting-in-review/

Bennett, J. (2016, December 8). *Everything you need to know about foraging for food in the wild.* Popular Mechanics. https://www.popularmechanics.com/adventure/outdoors/tips/a24203/eat-forage-food-wild-alone-history-channel/

Berens, C. (2017, November 7). *Checking things out: Public land in-season scouting methods.* Deer and Deer Hunting. https://www.deeranddeerhunting.com/content/articles/deer-news/checking-things-out-public-land-in-season-scouting-methods

Block, K., & Amundson, S. (2020, October 29). *Breaking news: The U.S. just delisted gray wolves so trophy hunters can kill them. A Humane World.* https://blog.humanesociety.org/2020/10/breaking-news-the-u-s-just-delisted-gray-wolves-so-trophy-hunters-can-kill-them.html

Bone Collector. (2018, March 26). *5 turkey hunting tactics to avoid getting busted.* Bone Collector. https://www.bonecollector.com/turkey-hunting-tactics-not-get-busted-spring/

BookYourHunt. (2020, November 15). *Moose hunting in the lower 48: Problems and opportunities.* BookYourHunt Blog. https://blog.bookyourhunt.com/2020/11/15/moose-hunting-in-the-lower-48-problems-and-opportunities/

Bourjaily, P. (2019, September 18). *A perfect use for the .410.* Field & Stream. https://www.fieldandstream.com/perfect-use-for-410-shotgun/

Brantley, W. (2020, May 26). *All about froggin'.* Realtree Camo. https://www.realtree.com/small-game-hunting/articles/all-about-froggin

Brown, M., & Flesher, J. (2019, March 14). *US moves to remove gray wolf protections.* Christian Science Monitor. https://www.csmonitor.com/Environment/2019/0314/US-moves-to-remove-gray-wolf-protections

Cantrell, J., & King, K. (2020, September 12). *Beginner's guide to deer hunting*. The Art of Manliness. https://www.artofmanliness.com/articles/a-primer-on-deer-hunting/

Capesquan. (2011, October 17). *How to create a lean-to shelter in the deciduous forest*. Instructables. https://www.instructables.com/How-to-create-a-lean-to-shelter-in-the-deciduous-f/

Castillo, E. (2019, April 24). *Understanding bird tracks and other game bird signs*. Project Upland. https://projectupland.com/culture/understanding-tracks-and-other-game-bird-signs/

De Jauregul, R. (n.d.). *Where & when do quails nest?* Pets on Mom.com. Retrieved May 12, 2021, from https://animals.mom.com/quails-nest-4742.html

Dick's Pro Tips. (2015, September 2). *A hunting checklist for beginners*. PRO TIPS by DICK'S Sporting Goods. https://protips.dickssportinggoods.com/sports-and-activities/hunt-and-fish/a-hunting-checklist-for-beginners

Dumbauld, B. (2019). *Top 10 outdoor survival tips*. Nwtf.org. https://www.nwtf.org/hunt/article/ten-outdoor-survival-tips

Elite Adventure Travel. (n.d.). *Beginners hunting*. Elite Travel. Retrieved May 17, 2021, from https://elitetravelgroup.net/beginners-hunting/

Evans, T. (2019, July 14). *Snapping turtles: 5 things you need to know*. The Indianapolis Star. https://www.indystar.com/story/news/local/2019/07/14/snapping-turtle-facts-indiana/1702908001/

EveryThingWhat. (2020, June 24). *Do snapping turtles poop?* https://everythingwhat.com/do-snapping-turtles-poop

FarWide. (2020, December 18). *Duck season – all you need to know | duck hunting*. https://www.farwide.com/duck-season-all-you-need-to-know/

Fenson, B. (2014, September 22). *How to spot-and-stalk greenheads with success*. Wildfowl. https://www.wildfowlmag.com/editorial/spot-stalks-greenheads/280230

Fleeman, K. (2017, November 3). *How to "prep" for a first hunt.* The Prepper Journal. https://theprepperjournal.com/2017/11/03/prep-first-hunt/?noamp=mobile

Florida Fish And Wildlife Conservation Commission. (n.d.). *Season dates and species.* Retrieved May 12, 2021, from https://myfwc.com/hunting/season-dates/

Fohrman, I. (2020, October 30). *The beginner's guide to hunting.* Outside. https://www.outsideonline.com/2422433/camping-mistakes-lessons-learned

Fratt, K. (2018, December 4). *11 edible mushrooms in the US (and how to tell they're not toxic).* Plantsnap. https://www.plantsnap.com/blog/edible-mushrooms-united-states/

Freel, T. (2015, August 13). *Hunting skills: 3 ways to mentally prepare yourself for a mountain hunt.* Outdoor Life. https://www.outdoorlife.com/blogs/game-changers/hunting-skills-3-ways-mentally-prepare-yourself-mountain-hunt/

Geiser, J. (2018, August 9). *Outdoors: Bullfrog season has arrived.* North Platte Nebraska's Newspaper. https://nptelegraph.com/sports/outdoors/outdoors-bullfrog-season-has-arrived/article_afab7110-9c51-11e8-a34b-6f553b2dd2c9.html

Gores, M. (2019, September 3). *How to prepare for hunting season – mental & physical training tips.* Campfire Collective. https://www.thecampfirecollective.com/blog/hunting-season-preparation/

Greenbelly. (2018, July 31). *Animal tracks identification guide.* Greenbelly Meals. https://www.greenbelly.co/pages/animal-tracks-identification-guide

Grouse Partnership. (n.d.). *Forest grouse.* The North American Grouse Partnership. Retrieved May 12, 2021, from http://www.grousepartners.org/forest-grouse

Hansen, T. (2019, July 19). *9 hard truths about hunting on public land.* Outdoor Life. https://www.outdoorlife.com/hard-truths-about-hunting-on-public-land/

Hart, D. (2019, December 20). *7 hot tips for hunting squirrels*. Www.themeateater.com. https://www.themeateater.com/hunt/squirrels/7-hot-tips-for-squirrel-hunting

Henderson, B. (2017, April 5). *A meateater's guide to eating invasive species*. Www.themeateater.com. https://www.themeateater.com/fish/freshwater/a-meateaters-guide-to-eating-invasive-species

Henderson, B. (2017, April 5). *A meateater's guide to eating invasive species*. Www.themeateater.com. https://www.themeateater.com/fish/freshwater/a-meateaters-guide-to-eating-invasive-species

Henderson, B. (2018, November 1). *Ask meateater: How do I get started hunting?* Www.themeateater.com. https://www.themeateater.com/hunt/small-game/ask-meateater-how-do-i-get-started-hunting

Hiking Guy. (2016, January 30). *Hiking for beginners: 11 essential tips*. https://hikingguy.com/how-to-hike/hiking-for-beginners-11-essential-tips/

Hunter, J. (2020, September 30). *5 ridiculously simple animal traps and snares for outdoor survival*. Primal Survivor. https://www.primalsurvivor.net/simple-animal-traps-snares/

Hunter-Ed. (n.d.-a). *National hunting laws and regulations*. Www.hunter-Ed.com. Retrieved May 6, 2021, from https://www.hunter-ed.com/national/hunting_law/

Hunter-Ed. (n.d.-b). *Steps you should take to prepare for a hunt*. Www.hunter-Ed.com. Retrieved May 17, 2021, from https://www.hunter-ed.com/national/studyGuide/Steps-You-Should-Take-to-Prepare-for-a-Hunt/201099_92916/

Hunting Fit. (2016, January 25). *7 steps to becoming a better hunter*. https://huntingfit.com/2016/01/25/7-steps-to-becoming-a-better-hunter/

Indiana Department of Natural Resources. (2021, January 29). *American bullfrog*. Fish & Wildlife. https://www.in.gov/dnr/fish-and-wildlife/wildlife-resources/animals/american-bullfrog/

Joe and Zach Survival. (2012, March 1). *How to set a rabbit snare* [Video]. YouTube. https://www.youtube.com/watch?v=aCs3QEIYYug

Johnston, J. (2020, June 25). *4 shooting drills to make you a better hunter.* Petersen's Hunting. https://www.petersenshunting.com/editorial/4-shooting-drills-to-make-you-better-hunter/377422

Krebs, N. (2020, June 3). *How to hunt: A step-by-step guide for new adult hunters.* Outdoor Life. https://www.outdoorlife.com/story/hunting/how-to-hunt-step-by-step-guide-for-new-adult-hunters/

Kwon, A. (2015, January 23). *The long of it: A sportsman's guide to the .22 rifle.* Gear Patrol. https://www.gearpatrol.com/outdoors/a117287/guide-to-the-22-rifle/

Linden, S. (2020, November 6). *Tips & tricks for more eastern ruffed grouse this season.* Game & Fish. https://www.gameandfishmag.com/editorial/tips-tricks-for-more-eastern-ruffed-grouse-this-season/385979

Lisson, R. (2017, August 25). *How to identify ruffed grouse habitat for hunting.* Project Upland. https://projectupland.com/grouse-species/ruffed-grouse-hunting/ruffed-grouse-habitat-2/

LiveOutdoors. (2012, August 29). *Going old-school for rabbits.* https://www.liveoutdoors.com/hunting/167337-going-old-school-for-rabbits/

LiveOutdoors. (2016, September 15). *4 tips for successful rabbit hunting.* https://www.liveoutdoors.com/hunting/241727-4-tips-for-successful-rabbit-hunting/

M4 Ranch Group. (2019, May 4). *What you need to know about hunting on private land.* https://m4ranchgroup.com/what-you-need-to-know-about-hunting-on-private-land/

MacKay, B., & MacKay, Ka. (2020, October 7). *Edible wild plants: 19 wild plants you can eat to survive in the wild.* The Art of Manliness. https://www.artofmanliness.com/articles/surviving-in-the-wild-19-common-edible-plants/

MacWelch, T. (2019, August 2). *How to identify tracks of 10 common North American species.* Outdoor Life. https://www.outdoorlife.com/identify-common-animal-tracks/

McGlothlin, J. (2020, November 17). *Tackling the hunter's first aid kit.* OnX Hunt. https://www.onxmaps.com/hunt/blog/tackling-hunter-first-aid-kits-what-to-include

Miller, B. (2018, February 1). *Take advantage of the post season to scout new hunting grounds.* Woods-n-Water News. https://woods-n-waternews.com/2018/02/01/articles-in-this-issue-i-2018-02-01-226521-112113-take-advantage-of-the-post-season-to-scout-new-hunting-grounds-html/

Mossy Oak. (2019, January 10). *Snapping turtles: How to catch, clean and cook.* Www.mossyoak.com. https://www.mossyoak.com/our-obsession/blogs/how-to/snapping-turtles-how-to-catch-clean-and-cook

Mr_Altitude. (2013, July 17). *Primitive fire starting: The bow drill.* Instructables. https://www.instructables.com/Fire-without-matches-or-metal/

National Wild Turkey Federation. (2002, April 17). *Field strategies: Reading turkey sign.* ESPN.com. https://www.espn.com/outdoors/hunting/news/story?page=h_fea_NWTF_reading-signs

Newhouse, R. (2020, September 18). *Essential hunting gear for beginners.* OnX Hunt. https://www.onxmaps.com/hunt/blog/hunting-gear-essentials

NH Fish and Game Department. (2019). *Snapping turtle.* State.nh.us. https://www.wildlife.state.nh.us/wildlife/profiles/snapping-turtle.html

NWTF. (n.d.). *Turkey hunting 101.* Www.nwtf.org. Retrieved May 12, 2021, from https://www.nwtf.org/hunt/article/turkey-hunting-101

Orvis. (n.d.). *Upland game birds of North America: An overview.* Www.orvis.com. Retrieved May 12, 2021, from https://www.orvis.com/upland-game-birds-of-north-america-an-overview.html

Philips, J. (n.d.-a). *How to hunt and take ducks by surprise: Day 1.* Www.nighthawkpublications.com. Retrieved May 15, 2021, from http://www.nighthawkpublications.com/journal/2013/02/journal_1.htm

Philips, J. (n.d.-b). *How to hunt and take ducks by surprise: Day 3.* Www.nighthawkpublications.com. Retrieved May 15, 2021, from http://www.nighthawkpublications.com/journal/2013/02/journal_3.htm

Philips, J. (n.d.-c). *How to hunt and take ducks by surprise: Day 4.* Www.nighthawkpublications.com. Retrieved May 15, 2021, from http://www.nighthawkpublications.com/journal/2013/02/journal_4.htm

Project Upland. (2019, April 28). *Bird hunting in Alabama, season dates, and bag limits - 2020 to 2021.* https://projectupland.com/rules-regulations-and-seasons/bird-hunting-in-alabama-2/

Reserve America. (2019, September 10). *How to get a hunting license.* Www.reserveamerica.com. https://www.reserveamerica.com/articles/fishing/how-to-get-a-hunting-license

Ridenour, T. (2017, February 7). *8 tips for public land hunts.* Bowhunting 360. https://bowhunting360.com/2017/02/07/8-tips-for-public-land-hunts/

Rinella, S. (2016, March 1). *A guide to hunting Hungarian partridge.* Www.themeateater.com. https://www.themeateater.com/hunt/upland-birds/a-guide-to-hunting-hungarian-partridge

Rinella, S. (2018a, January 16). *A guide to hunting cottontail rabbits.* Www.themeateater.com. https://www.themeateater.com/hunt/rabbits/a-guide-to-hunting-cottontail-rabbits

Rinella, S. (2018b, April 6). *The .22 rimfire.* Www.themeateater.com. https://www.themeateater.com/hunt/gear-hunt/what-you-need-to-know-about-22-ammunition

Rinella, S. (2018c, May 31). *A beginners guide to field survival kits for hunting.* Www.themeateater.com. https://www.themeateater.com/hunt/gear-hunt/a-beginners-guide-to-field-survival-kits-for-hunting

Rinella, S. (2018d, July 9). *A species profile on mallards.* Www.themeateater.com. https://www.themeateater.com/hunt/ducks/a-species-profile-on-mallards

Rinella, S. (2018e, December 4). *A guide to hunting wild turkey.* Www.themeateater.com. https://www.themeateater.com/hunt/wild-turkey/a-guide-to-hunting-wild-turkey

Rinella, S. (2019, February 5). *The complete guide to hunting squirrels.* Www.themeateater.com. https://www.themeateater.com/hunt/squirrels/a-guide-to-hunting-squirrels

Roy. (2018, October 3). *Do something new: Spot & stalk duck hunting.* Never a Goose Chase. https://neveragoosechase.com/2018/10/03/spot-stalk-duck-hunting/

Rude, L. (2020, December 4). DNR: *Gray wolf hunting season will start November 2021.* Channel3000.com. https://www.channel3000.com/dnr-gray-wolf-hunting-season-will-start-november-2021/

Scheels. (2016, August 10). *How to blow basic duck calls you need to know* [Video]. YouTube. https://www.youtube.com/watch?v=SMUft79pDOc

Shea, M. R. (n.d.). *10 super scouting tips.* Www.ducks.org. Retrieved May 13, 2021, from https://www.ducks.org/hunting/waterfowl-hunting-tips/ten-super-scouting-tips

Sigmon, M. R. (2004). Hunting and posting on private land in America. *Duke Law Journal*, 54, 549–585. https://scholarship.law.duke.edu/dlj/vol54/iss2/6

Spurlock, S. (2018, September 28). *The 30 day plan for a successful hunt.* GoHUNT. https://www.gohunt.com/read/skills/30-day-plan-for-a-successful-hunt#gs.1klkdz

Staff Compilation. (2014, October 16). *Moose hunting throughout the U.S.* The Norwegian American. https://www.norwegianamerican.com/moose-hunting-throughout-the-u-s/

Sutton, K. (2018, January 21). *How to get food when you're stranded and hungry.* Arkansas Online. https://www.arkansasonline.com/news/2018/jan/21/how-get-food-when-youre-stranded-and-hungry/

Sutton, K. (2018, January 21). *How to get food when you're stranded and hungry.* Arkansas Online. https://www.arkansasonline.com/news/2018/jan/21/how-get-food-when-youre-stranded-and-hungry/

SW-Virginia Outdoors. (2017, July 2). *Drying a slingshot fork* [Video]. YouTube. https://www.youtube.com/watch?v=f1es6pmbBZQ

Taylor, J. (2019, April 26). *The .410 shotgun: Everything you need to know about hunting and shooting with this sub-gauge.* Outdoor Life. https://www.outdoorlife.com/410-shotgun-everything-you-need-to-know-about-hunting-and-shooting-with-this-sub-gauge/

The Washington Department of Fish and Wildlife. (2021, January 12). *Forget the pear trees.* Medium. https://wdfw.medium.com/forget-the-pear-trees-693d8ff65d62

Trehearne, N. (2017, March 23). *How to scout for new western hunting grounds—in spring!* Outdoor Canada. https://www.outdoorcanada.ca/how-to-scout-for-new-hunting-groundsin-spring/

U.S. Department of the Interior. (2017, September 1). *Everything you need to know about hunting on public lands.* Www.doi.gov. https://www.doi.gov/blog/everything-you-need-know-about-hunting-public-lands

U.S. Fish and Wildlife Service. (2018). *Hunting.* Fws.gov. https://www.fws.gov/hunting/state-license.html

U.S. Fish and Wildlife Service. (2020, August 5). *Federal recreation lands pass.* Www.fws.gov. https://www.fws.gov/refuges/visit/federal-recreational-lands-pass.html

Videojug. (2012, March 24). *How to make your own slingshot* [Video]. YouTube. https://www.youtube.com/watch?v=eOuvLx_qU1o

Von Benedikt, J. (2017, July 13). *Best states to hunt for black bears.* Petersen's Hunting. https://www.petersenshunting.com/editorial/best-states-to-hunt-for-black-bears/272252

Von Malegowski. (2016, November 9). *How to start a fire with a cell phone battery* [Video]. YouTube. https://www.youtube.com/watch?v=i-47kTmBjH4

Weissinger, L. (n.d.). *Succulent snapper: How to catch snapping turtles.* Mother Earth News. Retrieved May 15, 2021, from https://www.motherearthnews.com/real-food/how-to-catch-snapping-turtles-zmaz80jazraw

Whitetail Properties. (2019, April 10). *Turkey calling tips | turkey sounds and what they mean* [Video]. YouTube. https://www.youtube.com/watch?v=zjE_kf--koY

Wilderness Today. (n.d.). *How to hunt quail 101: Upland bird hunting tips and tricks.* Wildernesstoday.com. Retrieved May 14, 2021, from https://wildernesstoday.com/quail-hunting/

Woods, S. (2016, February 13). *Paiute deadfall trap in action! Catching rats and mice. Bushcraft survival skills* [Video]. YouTube. https://www.youtube.com/watch?v=89GNUnn-8KQ

YourPelletGuns. (2020). *A comprehensive guide to the pellet gun (updated for 2020).* Yourpelletguns.com. https://yourpelletguns.com/pellet-gun-guide/

IMAGE REFERENCES

Alexas_Fotos. (2018, June 16). *Ducks pair mallards*. Pixabay. https://pixabay.com/photos/ducks-pair-mallards-colorful-3478009/

Audet, A. (2020, October 3). *Grouse animal nature ruffed*. Pixabay. https://pixabay.com/photos/grouse-animal-nature-ruffed-grouse-5623965/

Create219. (2017, June 3). *Turkey farm Australia*. Pixabay. https://pixabay.com/photos/turkey-farm-australia-feathers-2355465/

Crowhurst, S. (2020, April 16). *Bullfrog pond frog*. Pixabay. https://pixabay.com/photos/bullfrog-pond-frog-amphibian-5048916/

Hellinger14. (2012, June 20). *Rock partridge*. Pixabay. https://pixabay.com/photos/rock-partridge-bird-animals-nature-50362/

Manu Bird. (2017, September 8). *Californian quail*. Pixabay. https://pixabay.com/photos/californian-quail-new-zealand-bird-2727341/

Pixabay. (2016a, April 07). *Black and white squirrel*. Pexels. https://www.pexels.com/photo/nature-countryside-outside-cute-69447/

Pixabay. (2016b, Dec 09). *Close-up of rabbit on field*. Pexels. https://www.pexels.com/photo/close-up-of-rabbit-on-field-247373/

Simons, J. (2019, August 17). *Snapping turtle swamp*. Pixabay. https://pixabay.com/photos/snapping-turtle-turtle-swamp-4410907/